DAVID EDGAR

David Edgar took up playwriting after a short career in journalism.

His original plays for the theatre include *Death Story* for the Birmingham Repertory Theatre, *Saigon Rose* for the Traverse Theatre in Edinburgh, *Wreckers* for 7:84 England, *That Summer* for Hampstead Theatre and *Entertaining Strangers*, first as a community play for Dorchester and then at the National Theatre. His original plays for the RSC include

Destiny, Maydays and *Pentecost* (winner of the Evening Standard Best Play Award in 1995). *Pentecost* was the second of a series of plays about Eastern Europe after the Cold War, following *The Shape of the Table* (NT) and preceding *The Prisoner's Dilemma* (RSC). *Continental Divide*, his two-play cycle about American politics, comprising the plays *Mothers Against* and *Daughters of the Revolution*, was premiered at

the Oregon Shakespeare Festival and Berkeley Rep, before transferring to the Birmingham Repertory Theatre and the Barbican Centre in London. *Playing with Fire*, premiered at the National Theatre, marked a return to the subject matter explored in *Destiny*: race and multiculturalism in British society.

His other adaptations include *Mary Barnes* for the Birmingham Repertory Theatre; *The Jail Diary* of .... and a Tony Award-winning adapt   for the RSC; and *Albert S*   a Sereny's biography.

David Edgar has also v   wrote the screenplay fo   ..... *Lady Jane*. He founded and directed Britain's first postgraduate course in playwriting at the University of Birmingham from 1989 to 1999; he was appointed professor in 1995.

Other Adaptations in this Series

DAVID EDGAR

DR JEKYLL
AND MR HYDE

a new version of the novel by
ROBERT LOUIS STEVENSON

NICK HERN BOOKS
London
www.nickhernbooks.co.uk

A Nick Hern Book

Dr Jekyll and Mr Hyde based on the story by
Robert Louis Stevenson first published in Great Britain
as a paperback original in 1996 by Nick Hern Books Ltd,
14 Larden Road, London W3 7ST

Reprinted 2005

Dr Jekyll and Mr Hyde copyright © 1996 by David Edgar

An earlier version of this play, *The Strange Case of Dr Jekyll
and Mr Hyde*, was published in 1992

Front cover photograph by Robert Workman from the
Birmingham Repertory Company's production of
Dr Jekyll and Mr Hyde

Typeset by Country Setting, Kingsdown, Kent CT14 8ES
Printed by Athenaeum Press, Gateshead, Tyne & Wear

A CIP catalogue record for this book is available from
the British Library

ISBN-13   978 1 85459 297 2
ISBN-10   1 85459 297 1

'In 1885 Gilles de Tourette, a pupil of Charcot, described the astonishing syndrome which now bears his name. "Tourette's syndrome" as it was immediately dubbed, is characterised by an excess of nervous energy, and a great production and extravagance of strange motions and notions: tics, jerks, mannerisms, grimaces, noises, curses, involuntary imitations and compulsions of all sorts, with an odd elfin humour and a tendency to antic and outlandish kinds of play . . . it was clear to Tourette and his peers, that this syndrome was a sort of possession by primitive impulses and urges.'

Oliver Sacks, *The Man Who Mistook His Wife For A Hat*

'Certain scandals about London which were revealed by the Pall Mall Gazette in 1885 seemed at the time to prove that the attribution of sadism as an English characteristic was by no means merely arbitrary. In its issues of July 6th, 7th, 8th, and 10th, 1885, there was published in this paper a series of articles entitled "The Maiden Tribute of Modern Babylon", in which were exposed the results of an inquiry into youthful prostitution in London. The moving spirit of this campaign, which was intended to provoke Government measures for the protection of minors, was the journalist W.T. Stead . . . The paragraphs which made the greatest impression were those which dealt with sadism – "Why the cries of the victims are not heard", and "Strapping girls down": these paragraphs were considerably abridged when the collected articles were put on sale.'

Mario Praz, *The Romantic Agony*

In the autumn of 1885 Robert Louis Stevenson was living at Bournemouth, where he dreamt – and then wrote – *The Strange Case of Dr Jekyll and Mr Hyde.*

From Stevenson, to Katherine

From me, to Kate

Introduction

At the beginning of the 80s, I wrote an extremely long adaptation of a huge early Victorian novel for the Royal Shakespeare Company. There seemed to be a symmetry about the fact that at the end of the 80s I was working on if not a short then at least a reasonably-lengthed version of a novella written towards the end of Victoria's reign.

The contrast between the two works could not on the surface be more stark. In addition to the fact that *Nicholas Nickleby* is 850 pages long and *Jekyll and Hyde* less than 80, the first novel is sprawling, linear, teeming, comic and picaresque, whereas the second is tight, serious, chronologically complex and set in a strangely desolate London, peopled by lonely bachelors proceeding through empty streets at dead of night.

But there are comparisons, parallels and mirrorings. Both novels are illuminated by their full titles ('The *Life and Adventures* of Nicholas Nickleby'; 'The *Strange Case* of Dr Jekyll and Mr Hyde'). Both were written very fast: in Dickens' case, to satisfy an increasingly insatiable public; in Stevenson's, to answer the even more pressing demands of his butcher. And both centre on relationships between a whole person and a kind of half-completed double: though Smike is the better part of his cousin Nicholas, while Hyde is Jekyll's nightmare.

And in retrospect, it can be seen that they both relate to the great central event of 19th-century Britain, which was the seemingly definitive triumph of industrial capitalism between the end of the 1840s (ten years after *Nickleby*) and the middle 1870s (about a decade before *Jekyll*). The characteristic of this central period was a seemingly limitless confidence, not just about the powers of men to transform their fortunes through industry, but also about the capacity of sensible people to redress the social problems that those powers had brought into being.

In anticipation of this event, Dickens is expressing fears that the great move from the country to the city was already threatening the social fabric, leaving the newly uprooted urban middle classes (in particular) disoriented and scared; while at the end of the long boom, similar fears are being expressed, but in darker form. The social and financial threats to Mrs Nickleby, Miss la Creevy and the Kenwigs family are real enough, but they are graspable, and responsive to human treatment. The demons that haunt Henry Jekyll are altogether more threatening. They are about a world in which unbelievable riches have failed to answer the most pressing longings of the human heart, and in which men who promised to master everything have found themselves unable to control even their own instincts.

If *Nickleby* and *Jekyll* bookend the heroic period of what we think of as high Victorian England, then my two adaptations frame an echoing period of our own history. The RSC's *Nickleby* was so successful in 1980 because, a year into Thatcher, our audiences wanted to be assured that there was more to life than money. *Jekyll* was written in 1885, at a time when a depraved and degenerate urban underclass (then called the Remnant) is thought to be beyond social redemption, when revelations of child prostitution shock the nation, syphilis is feared to be reaching uncontrollable proportions and the homeless are camping out in Trafalgar Square.

Also, *Jekyll* is written at a time when the approaching end of a century appears to be heralding a period of irretrievable cultural breakdown. Contemporary Britons too feel themselves threatened by a collapse of values, the breakdown of family, the riotous appetites of an underclass and the consequences of uncontrolled international migration, and in consequence seek to secure and buttress the barriers between the genders, the classes and the races. Similarly, the men of Stevenson's world felt threatened by invasion from the East End, infection by homosexual decadence and contamination by the mulatto masses of the Empire.

It is also the era in which men started to fight back against the New Woman. This is seen most starkly in the extraordinary literary change that occurs with the death of George Eliot in 1880 and the almost immediate substitution of the one-volume, boys' story for the three-volume family saga that had dominated fiction since Jane Austen. Like the buddy movies of today, the male pairings at the centre of late Victorian thrillers (from Holmes and Watson on) are clearly seeking to escape a usually unmentioned but ever-present threat.

Since 1887, almost all the dramatisations have lopped 20 years off Dr Jekyll's age and given him a fiancée or a girlfriend (often with

a disapproving father for Hyde to murder). I have returned to
Stevenson's original world of crusty, ageing masculinity. But
I wanted to show the feminine threat that is implicit in the novel
(in which, incidentally, there is no named woman character at all),
and the best way of doing both was to give him not a fiancée but a
sister, and to make her an example of those very forces that were
so alarming men like Henry Jekyll.

In returning to the ambience of the original, I was I suppose
engaging in an act of restoration, stripping away the varnish to
reveal a great work in its true colours. Certainly this is how I have
always seen the adaptation of *Nicholas Nickleby*. I am however
less convinced that that was quite what I was doing here. For in
adapting something like *Jekyll and Hyde* one must deal not only
with the original, but also with what has been subsequently done to
it. I may try to forget Jekyll's myriad fiancées, but my audiences
won't. I thus found myself adapting not only Stevenson, but also
Mansfield (the 1887 play), Mamoulian (the 1931 movie), Fleming
(the 1941 Spencer Tracy version) and indeed a clutch of contemporary re-readings, from Valerie Martin's chilling novel *Mary
Reilly* (since adapted for the screen by Christopher Hampton) via
at least one other current British stage version (by Robin Brooks
for Empty Space) to – rumour had it – no fewer than three
American musicals.

In one crucial respect, however, my adaptation departed from
tradition, by separating out the two central characters. In the RSC
production of my first version, Roger Allam and Simon Russell
Beale brought huge intelligence and attack to playing the two sides
of a single personality. But in addition to denying the audience the
pleasure of seeing one man turn himself into another before their
very eyes, we discovered that the theatre's remorseless corporeality
prevented the audience from making the essential leap of belief.
Try as we might to convince them that they were seeing a battle
inside a single soul, what was actually in front of them were two
men in Victorian clothes having an argument in a laboratory.
Accordingly, when Bill Alexander invited me to rework the play
for the Birmingham Repertory Theatre, I decided to revert to the
more traditional model. It was no surprise to either of us when
David Schofield rose magnificently to the challenge.

I have thus been lucky enough to have two goes at one of the great
adaptation opportunities (and challenges) of the last hundred years.
For the adaptor, the essential difference between *Nickleby* and
Jekyll is that the former is viewed (unjustly) as a minor work and

the latter is one of the best known plots (if not texts) of the nineteenth century. But for that very reason it seems worth revisiting. There are, as I've argued, particular reasons why Stevenson's 'fine bogey tale' seems to speak particularly to our flawed and fractured times (the idea that letting one's appetites hang out might be ultimately suicidal would not, I think, have meant much in the mid-60s). But the main point is that the theatre should be in the business of re-reading not its own past texts but those from other sources – something the cinema has always understood.

Oscar Wilde believed that 'it is only the unimaginative who ever invent. The true artist is known by the use he makes of what he annexes, and he annexes everything'. I am not entirely convinced of the truth of this in all respects, but it is clearly the adaptor's creed. And, as it happens, Wilde said it in the early summer of 1885.

David Edgar

David Edgar's adaptation of Stevenson's novel, *The Strange Case of Dr Jekyll and Mr Hyde*, was first staged by the Royal Shakespeare Company at the Barbican Theatre, London, on 21 November 1991. Press night was 27 November. The cast, in order of appearance, was:

GABRIEL JOHN UTTERSON, *a lawyer*	Oliver Ford Davies
RICHARD ENFIELD	Michael Bott
KATHERINE URQUART, *Jekyll's sister*	Pippa Guard
LUCY, } *her children*	Ellie Beaven/Lilly Gallafent
CHARLES, } *her children*	Robert Jones/Mark Turnley
ANNIE LODER, *her maid*	Katrina Levon
DR HENRY JEKYLL, FRS	Roger Allam
POOLE, *his butler*	John Bott
DR HASTIE LANYON	Alec Linstead
MR HYDE	Simon Russell Beale
A MAID	Lucy Slater
SIR DANVERS CAREW, MP	Leonard Kavanagh
A PARSON	John Hodgkinson
RAILWAY GUARD	Troy Webb
BOATMEN	Simon Elliott
	Troy Webb
BOATWOMAN	Corinne Harris
CHILDREN	Natalia Cerqueira
	Kendal Gaw, Kitty Healey,
	Johannah Playford

Directed by Peter Wood
Set designed by Carl Toms
Costumes designed by Johan Engels
Lighting by David Hersey
Music by Robert Lockhart

This fully revised and partially re-written version, now called *Dr Jekyll and Mr Hyde*, was first performed at the Birmingham Repertory Theatre from 28 June 1996. Press night was 2 July. The cast, in order of appearance, was:

GABRIEL JOHN UTTERSON	Paul Webster
RICHARD ENFIELD, PARSON	Paul Connolly
LUCY, MAID, WOMAN *on platform*	Verity Bray
CHARLES, *Lucy's brother*	Christopher Trezise
KATHERINE URQUART, *their mother*	Francesca Ryan
ANNIE LODER, *a parlourmaid*	Annie Farr
DR HENRY JEKYLL, EDWARD HYDE	David Schofield
POOLE, *Dr Jekyll's butler*	Geoffrey Freshwater
DR LANYON, SIR DANVERS CAREW	Desmond Jordan

Directed by Bill Alexander
Designed by Ruari Murchinson
Lighting designed by Tim Mitchell
Fight directed by Malcolm Ranson
Music composed by Jonathan Goldstein, *played by* Simon Murray
Dialect coaching by Jill McCollough
Stage managed by Sally Isern, Lisa Buckley, Jonathan Smith-Howard

DR JEKYLL AND MR HYDE

Characters

GABRIEL JOHN UTTERSON
RICHARD ENFIELD
LUCY
CHARLES, *her brother*
KATHERINE URQUART, *their mother*
ANNIE LODER, *a parlourmaid*
DR HENRY JEKYLL
POOLE, *his butler*
DR HASTIE LANYON
MR HYDE
A MAID
SIR DANVERS CAREW MP
A PARSON
A RAILWAYMAN
A WOMAN *on the platform*

ENFIELD *doubles with the* PARSON, LANYON *doubles with* CAREW *and the* RAILWAYMAN. *The* MAID *and the* WOMAN *on the platform could double with* LUCY. Dr JEKYLL *must double with* Mr HYDE.

ACT ONE

Scene One

*London: a chill and gloomy autumn afternoon. At one side of the
stage,* GABRIEL JOHN UTTERSON *appears; at the other, his
cousin* RICHARD ENFIELD. UTTERSON *is a lawyer in late
middle-age,* ENFIELD *the man of fashion is younger.*

ENFIELD. Mr Utterson the lawyer was a man of rugged
countenance, that was never lighted by a smile; Cold, scanty
and embarrassed in discourse; backward in sentiment; lean,
long, dusty, dreary . . . and yet somehow lovable.

UTTERSON *looks quizzically over to* ENFIELD.

He was austere with himself; drank gin when he was alone, to
mortify a taste for vintages; and though he enjoyed the theatre,

UTTERSON. had not crossed the doors of one for twenty years.

ENFIELD. His friends were those of his own blood or those whom
he had known the longest; his affections,

UTTERSON. like ivy,

ENFIELD. were the growth of time, they implied no aptness in the
object.

UTTERSON. Hence, no doubt, the bond that united him to Mr
Richard Enfield, his distant kinsman, the well-known man
about town.

ENFIELD *smiles.*

ENFIELD. It was a nut to crack for many, what these two could
see in each other or what subject they could find in common. It
was reported by those who encountered them on their Sunday
walks, that they said nothing, looked singularly dull, and hailed
with obvious relief the appearance of a friend. But for all that,
the two men put the greatest store by these excursions, and not
only set aside occasions of pleasure,

UTTERSON. but even resisted the calls of business,

ENFIELD/UTTERSON. that they might enjoy them uninterrupted.

UTTERSON. It chanced on one of these rambles that their way led
them down a dingy by-street in a quiet quarter of London.

ENFIELD. Where the line of frontages was broken by a block of building with a blistered door –

UTTERSON. – bearing in every feature the marks of prolonged and sordid negligence.

ENFIELD. Did you ever remark that door?

UTTERSON. Mr Enfield said.

ENFIELD. It is connected in my mind with a very strange occurrence.

UTTERSON. And what was that? Mr Utterson replied.

ENFIELD. Well, it was this way. It must have been a week or so ago, I was coming home from some place at the end of the world, past twelve on a foggy night, and the streets all empty as a church. Until that is, I was overtaken by a young man of – well, a rather raffish, even primitive appearance, brandishing a cane, who was stomping at a breakneck speed towards the corner, where a wretched waif of ten or twelve or so was standing, selling sorry trifles from a tray.

Between the two men, we begin to sense a third figure.

UTTERSON. I'm sorry, you said 'young'?

ENFIELD. Yes, no more than twenty-two or three. And then –

UTTERSON. And with a cane?

ENFIELD. Yes, certainly, with a silver top. And then –

UTTERSON. And you said, this corner, and this door?

Slight pause.

ENFIELD. I did. Why do you ask?

UTTERSON. For Mr Utterson the lawyer knew that door, and where it led, and those who dwelt beyond it . . .

ENFIELD. And thus was able to connect his cousin's story with a malignant chain of circumstance which had begun some months before,

UTTERSON. Of which he was by then but at the doorway of suspicion.

And now we see that the third figure is a little WAIF, *with a makeshift tray of paltry things. As she speaks, the lights on* ENFIELD *and* UTTERSON *slowly fade to darkness.*

THE WAIF. Lights! Box of lights! Fine cotton thread! Best lampblack!

She 'sees' a MAN *approach, in the darkness, and turns to one side.*

Sir, a box of lights? or a tin of lampblack? Might you be
needing of a ha'penny's of black today?

We imagine the MAN *crosses in front of her as if to pass on.*

'Cos I'll be honest with you, sir, I needs the ha'penny.

We imagine the MAN *turns back and starts to walk towards the
girl.*

So I would take it awful kindly, sir. If you could see your way
sir. Even just a stick of kindling or a twist of tea.

She takes a match from a match box and prepares to light it.

Or a box of lights, sir?

She strikes the match. We see the moustached face of a SMALL
MAN, *leering through the darkness.*

Light?

*Then, suddenly, from the other side, a shaft of light from an
opening door. A* SECOND MAN *entering.*

SECOND MAN. What's this? What's going on?

The WAIF *turns to the* SECOND MAN.

THE WAIF. Oh, Uncle *Henry.*

SECOND MAN. What on earth –

SMALL MAN. Oh, rats.

As the SMALL MAN *leaves the* WAIF *we hear a* WOMAN'*s
voice.*

WOMAN. Charles.

The SMALL MAN *pulls open heavy curtains, flooding the
stage with light.*

SMALL MAN. Well, it's all spoilt.

Scene Two

*Now we pick up the situation: we are in the drawing room of a
country house, towards the end of a late summer afternoon. A
central alcove has been turned into a little theatrical booth, hung
with curtains. To the side, partly concealed by the arch of the
alcove, a maid stands on a chair with an oil-lamp, masked to
throw light on the* WAIF, *whose real name is* LUCY. *Her 13-year-
old brother* CHARLES *played the* SMALL MAN – *in cloak, top
hat and false moustache, all of them too big for him; the now
descending maid is 16-year-old* ANNIE; *and the rehearsal was*

being watched by CHARLES's *mother* KATHERINE, *who is in her early middle age. The curtains that* CHARLES *has pulled back expose french windows; we see that the room is untidy, full of toys, and contains a piano, a portrait photograph of two children –* CHARLES *and* LUCY *– and a painting of a fierce Scottish gentleman against a landscape background. The intruder is* KATHERINE's *older brother,* HENRY JEKYLL.

JEKYLL. What's spoilt? Katherine?

    KATHERINE *moves towards her brother.*

KATHERINE. It was a play the children were rehearsing, to perform to you.

LUCY. As a *surprise.*

KATHERINE. As a surprise.

JEKYLL. Well, I am so very sorry, I . . .

KATHERINE. And you were supposed to be upstairs writing letters.

CHARLES. He was supposed to be asleep!

JEKYLL. Asleep?

KATHERINE. That's what we thought you meant.

CHARLES. And now the whole thing's *spoilt.*

    He throws his top hat and cloak aside, and pulls off his fake moustache. A moment.

JEKYLL. Uh, if truth be told, I hardly –

LUCY. It's no use. If it isn't a *surprise.*

    She puts her tray down and runs out. KATHERINE *takes a previously rolled cigarette from a box.*

KATHERINE. Annie. I think perhaps it's time for the children to have tea.

LUCY (*calls from off*). I don't want any tea!

ANNIE. Yes, ma'am.

    She follows LUCY *out.*

KATHERINE. And Charles, you'd better tidy up.

CHARLES. No!

KATHERINE. Charles.

CHARLES (*grumpily*). All right.

    KATHERINE *goes a little apart to smoke her cigarette.*
    CHARLES *goes upstage, returns the lamp to its proper place,*

and begins to take down the curtaining. JEKYLL *decides to help.*

JEKYLL. So. There's this matchgirl, and this sinister cloaked figure . . .

CHARLES *decides to accept the olive branch.*

CHARLES. Who, using his wicked wiles, entices her into an alley where she is found, in the chill light of morning, murdered horribly.

JEKYLL. I see.

CHARLES. Initially, the police look out for a deranged ruffian or ne'erdowell. But increasingly they suspect the fiend in human shape to be an important member of society.

JEKYLL. The fiend in human shape.

CHARLES. Correct. But then –

KATHERINE. But then if you tell him everything then it really will be spoilt. Whereas you could start off again where you left off.

CHARLES. With the enticement.

He finishes returning the curtaining to rights.

KATHERINE. Yes. Tomorrow.

CHARLES. Oh. All right.

ANNIE *appears to summon* CHARLES *to tea. Speaking from the play:*

CHARLES. By Jove, lovely missy, 'tis a cruel night for such a one as you to be about –

ANNIE (*correcting*). 'Abroad'. And it be 'pretty missy'.

CHARLES. Come, where I may peruse your fine wares better. Come, come, come.

As he goes, with a grin:

To be continued in our next sensational edition.

CHARLES *and* ANNIE *have gone.* KATHERINE *has finished her cigarette, she comes back into the body of the room. She picks up* CHARLES*'s cloak, folds it, puts it and the top hat tidily on the seat of the winged chair.*

KATHERINE. They get it from the penny dreadfuls.

JEKYLL. Where?

KATHERINE. I believe the source to be the gardener's boy.

JEKYLL. Was that not father's?

KATHERINE (*with the top hat*). Yes it was.

JEKYLL. Katherine. Tomorrow I must go.

KATHERINE. Oh, must you?

JEKYLL. Yes.

KATHERINE. Then today we must discover why you came.

Pause.

JEKYLL. What do you mean?

KATHERINE. I mean, it's charming that you've come to visit us. It's what, two years since father died? And my Charles the February after. Lucy thought you lived in mourning clothes.

JEKYLL. I'm sorry.

KATHERINE. So there has been much speculation, as you might imagine. Lucy, for example, was of the opinion that your flight from London life was occasioned by the reappearance of a lover of your youth, now a Russian countess but when you first knew her but an humble chambermaid.

JEKYLL. Well, really.

KATHERINE. While Charles is firmly of the view that you yourself have committed some dreadful murder and dismembered the remains, but were fearful that the police were on your track. He said all doctors were dismemberers and grave-robbers. The fact is apparently well known.

JEKYLL. Well, is it now.

KATHERINE. So, then, your imminent return? To give your heart up to your countess or your self up to the police? Or just a night out with some bravoes at the Tivoli?

JEKYLL. I have to give a lecture on the cure of scarlet fever to the Ladies' Sanitary Association.

KATHERINE. And what's your programme? Better drains or sober living?

JEKYLL. Both helpful doubtless. But eventually. I'm sure, some kind of pill.

KATHERINE. But surely *then* with a gang of libertines to Willis's?

JEKYLL. No, but I am pledged to entertain two old, dull friends, in my old dull house, who meet together for the same dull conversation every second Friday of the month.

Enter ANNIE *with tea on a tray or trolley.*

JEKYLL. For I assure you, there's a great deal more loose living goes on, behind country hedgerows between stablelads and dairymaids than anywhere I go.

KATHERINE. You sound a little jealous.

JEKYLL. Well, that wasn't my intent.

ANNIE *coughs.*

KATHERINE. Ah. Tea.

ANNIE. Yes, m'm.

ANNIE *sets up tea and pours cups for* KATHERINE *and* JEKYLL.

JEKYLL. So, may I ask, which of these elegant hypotheses –

KATHERINE. Henry, I don't need a hypothesis, elegant or otherwise. I know why you're here.

JEKYLL. Oh yes?

KATHERINE. You're after one of father's books. You've been looking along bookshelves every since you came.

Pause.

ANNIE. Um, milk, sir?

JEKYLL. Yes. Yes, please.

KATHERINE. But I have to tell you, if it's something scientific, then it's in the attic. In a box. Yes, thank you, Annie.

ANNIE. Ma'am.

She goes out. Pause.

KATHERINE. So, have I hit the target?

JEKYLL. Katherine, I came because I was invited.

KATHERINE (*gesturing to the toys*). And bearing music boxes, spinning tops and model grenadiers.

JEKYLL. Why, were they too extravagant?

KATHERINE. What, like that dreadful ditty of papa's?

JEKYLL. What 'dread-'

KATHERINE. 'For every something something . . . spurned, a ton of godly treasure's earned'.

JEKYLL. It's 'for every earthly pleasure spurned'.

KATHERINE. Yes, right. Or rather, wrong. In this household, we don't take that view. Any more, of course, than he did.

JEKYLL *looks away.*

Which is why, if all those dusty books and ledgers give you any pleasure, terrestial or otherwise, you must have them.

JEKYLL. Katherine, father left his personal effects to you.

KATHERINE. Yes, which was wrong of him. And cruel. Knowing how much they'd mean to you.

Pause.

JEKYLL. Well, naturally, if you've no use for the medical –

KATHERINE. Not just the medical. The literature. And there's shelves of glasswork and ceramics. And that's not all.

She's going upstage. JEKYLL *thinks she's going to give him the hat.*

JEKYLL. Um, Katherine, he was three sizes larger –

But KATHERINE *meant the portrait.*

KATHERINE. I want you to have this. I want you to have father's portrait. I'll go further. I insist.

JEKYLL. Katherine, I obviously can't.

KATHERINE. Whyever not?

JEKYLL. Not least, because it's of our father, but it's by your husband.

KATHERINE. Never liked it much.

JEKYLL. Who never liked it?

KATHERINE. Neither of 'em. Charles thought it was sub-Gainsborough and papa said that it made him look like he was wanted by the police.

JEKYLL. What's wrong with Gainsborough?

KATHERINE. Charles took the view all Georgian art aspires to the condition of upholstery.

JEKYLL. Indeed?

KATHERINE. It was a kind of – olive branch.

JEKYLL. I see.

KATHERINE. But I remember, at Glencourse, on the very morning of the funeral, you standing in the Great Hall, looking up at this. And you turned to me and said you'd always loved him more than any other living creature. So it's yours.

JEKYLL. But it looks so right here.

KATHERINE. No it doesn't. What looks so right here is that portrait of the children. Don't you think?

KATHERINE *leads* JEKYLL *to the photograph.*

JEKYLL. I didn't know that Charles took photographs.

KATHERINE. He didn't. I do.

JEKYLL. What?

KATHERINE. It's my new pursuit. The Christmas after Charles died, I gave myself a Beck.

She goes to the photograph.

JEKYLL. A what?

KATHERINE. Oh, Henry, really. It's a reflex twin lens camera with roller-blind type shutter mechanism, and a quarter dry-plate magazine attached. So, quite the latest thing in all departments. What d'you think?

JEKYLL. It's – a very touching composition.

KATHERINE. Well, I hope it's more than touching. It was intended to be true.

JEKYLL. You think one sees the truth of people in their faces?

KATHERINE. Why else look into the mirror.

JEKYLL moves aside, and picks up the spinning top. Ruminatively:

JEKYLL. Well, I'd have thought, to see the opposite. Surely it's where we practise our deceits and our disguises.

KATHERINE. But that's exactly how one tells the truth of things. The opposite way round. The wrong way up.

Slight pause.

I'm told that everybody has a kind of – shadow in the mirror. Another self, which our conscious minds refuse to recognise.

JEKYLL. Oh, Katherine.

KATHERINE. Papa believed it. That's what he was investigating.

JEKYLL. Oh, is that so?

KATHERINE. But he stopped when he got scared where it might lead. He was frightened he might find the soul. Or worse, that he might open up the door marked 'soul', and find an empty room.

Slight pause.

So, is it anything – particular, you're looking for?

JEKYLL smiles and shrugs, turning the top in his hands.

Oh, go on, Henry. Try. You're dying to.

JEKYLL. I – what?

> KATHERINE *nods at the top.* JEKYLL *gives a slight smile.*
> *Then he starts the top. It hums.*

KATHERINE. You see. The truth will out eventually. It all
depends on the extent of the exposure.

> *Enter* LUCY *and* CHARLES. LUCY *sees* JEKYLL *with her*
> *top.*

LUCY. Mama. That is my top.

KATHERINE. I was showing it to Uncle Henry. Who in this
matter is as you will recollect your benefactor.

LUCY. Oh, well, that's all right then.

KATHERINE. Have you have your tea?

CHARLES. We have.

LUCY. Mama, Charles tells us we can do the play.

KATHERINE. But not just now.

LUCY. Whyever not?

KATHERINE. Because it's late. And Uncle Henry's tired.

CHARLES. He doesn't look tired. Are you tired, Uncle?

JEKYLL. Well, I . . .

LUCY. I bet he isn't too tired for a game.

> JEKYLL *looks at* KATHERINE.

KATHERINE. It's up to you.

JEKYLL. What game?

LUCY. Backgammon. Hazard.

CHARLES. No.

LUCY. Why not?

CHARLES. He means a proper game. Tipcat. Or grandma's
footsteps. Or –

LUCY. Or hide and seek.

> *Slight pause. They look at* JEKYLL.

CHARLES. It's unfair. He doesn't know the house.

LUCY. He is a grown-up.

> JEKYLL *spreads his hands.*

CHARLES. All right, then. Count up to a hundred.

LUCY. And don't *cheat.*

CHARLES *and* LUCY *exit.*

JEKYLL. One two three four . . . They're charming children.

KATHERINE. When they get their way.

JEKYLL. All children can be selfish. Nine, ten, eleven –

KATHERINE. How unlike grown-ups.

JEKYLL. And it can't have been too easy for you. Fourteen, fifteen!

KATHERINE. No. No, to lose a father to a husband, then to lose both to the grave within a year. It takes some getting over. As you might imagine.

JEKYLL. Yes.

Slight pause.

Uh, twenty – three, four, five –

KATHERINE. Henry, I'd leave two minutes and get after them.

JEKYLL. Isn't that cheating?

KATHERINE. Only yourself. A hundred is about a minute and a half. So were you never tempted?

JEKYLL. Tempted?

KATHERINE. To 'a wee wife and some bairns'?

JEKYLL. Oh, Katherine, I hardly think so.

KATHERINE. 'Oh Katherine I hardly think so'. Oh, come on. Once you forget you're Dr E. Henry Jekyll FRS. You could be more or less an ordinary human being.

JEKYLL *makes no response.*

So in the morning I will have papa well wrapped up for the journey.

JEKYLL. Katherine –

KATHERINE. And you'll take the books, of course. And please, the glassware and the furniture.

KATHERINE *goes to the piano.*

Though to be honest, for the children, I would like to keep the piano.

JEKYLL. Katherine, there's no –

KATHERINE. At least until –

KATHERINE *stumbles, falling on the keyboard of the piano.*

JEKYLL. Uh – Katherine –

KATHERINE. Oh, lord. Oh, lord, my head –

JEKYLL *looks to the door.*

JEKYLL. Um, should I –

KATHERINE *is recovering.*

KATHERINE. No. No, it's all right.

JEKYLL. You're sure?

KATHERINE. Yes. Yes. I just felt, uh – a mite vertiginous.

JEKYLL. Vertiginous?

KATHERINE. Well, dizzy.

Pause.

JEKYLL. Still?

KATHERINE. Well, yes.

Pause. She goes and takes another cigarette from her box.

But very rarely now.

Slight pause. JEKYLL goes and closes the keyboard lid.

JEKYLL. Please keep the piano. I haven't played a note for thirty years.

Slight pause.

Indeed, since we – last played together.

KATHERINE. Well, imagine that.

Slight pause.

I'm sure that's your two minutes, Henry.

She goes out. JEKYLL looks round. He sees the top hat and cloak. He puts them on. They're a bit big for him. He is about to go when ANNIE enters to tidy up. She doesn't see JEKYLL. Picking up a music box, she sets off the tune. She begins to dance. The dance turns into a spin. Suddenly she sees JEKYLL in the hat and cloak and screams.

ANNIE. Oh. Oh, sir . . .

JEKYLL. Ninety-nine, one hundred. I'm coming!

JEKYLL *marches out of the room, bumping into KATHERINE coming in. ANNIE shuts the music box.*

KATHERINE. Dr Jekyll's playing with the children.

ANNIE. Yes, ma'am. I knows.

KATHERINE. Hence the strange behaviour and the three-size larger hat.

ANNIE. Oh, I knows stranger, ma'am.

KATHERINE. I'm sure you do.

ANNIE's looking up at the portrait.

ANNIE. So do there be – a likeness? Like, in real life?

KATHERINE. A likeness?

She realises ANNIE'*s looking at the portrait.*

Ah. I see.

Slight pause.

Annie, our father was a brilliant man. But he was also
something of a 'fiend in human form'. My brother, happily, has
turned out to be neither. But he found it – he still finds it – very
hard.

She makes to go. ANNIE *calls after.*

ANNIE. Well, if I was him, I knows where I'd be looking, ma'am.

KATHERINE. Oh, yes? Where's that?

ANNIE. The attic.

Scene Three

We hear JEKYLL'*s voice immediately. Then lights come up on
Paddington Station.* JEKYLL'*s luggage, including the wrapped
portrait, is loaded on a trolley. Beside it,* JEKYLL *stands in a light
overcoat reading a large notebook; there is a gladstone bag –
containing other notebooks – on the platform beside him.*

JEKYLL. 'In his paper, A.J.G. claimed that oriental shamans are
so persuaded of the essential dualism of the human personality
that they have found a method to effect an actual corporeal
transformation. By this means, so it is maintained, man's basic
instincts might be split off from that higher part which
necessarily represses them.

JEKYLL looks up for a moment. Then back to the notebook.

'In my view, "necessarily" and "properly" '.

JEKYLL smiles. His old butler POOLE *appears with the last
of the cases.* JEKYLL *reads on.*

'For completion of the record, nonetheless, I append the
formula for both -'

POOLE *draws his presence to his master's attention.*

POOLE. So sir. You had a pleasant stay in Dorsetshire?

JEKYLL puts the notebook in the gladstone bag.

JEKYLL. Yes, thank you, Poole. But I fear I have returned a little heavy laden.

POOLE looks at the luggage.

POOLE. Yes, sir.

JEKYLL. My sister wishes to divest herself of items of our father's property.

POOLE. I see.

JEKYLL. And indeed his person.

POOLE. I beg your pardon sir?

JEKYLL. That is my father.

POOLE. Yes, sir. Do you have any notion where you'd like him hung?

POOLE picks up the gladstone.

JEKYLL (*suddenly*). No, Poole, leave that.

POOLE. I beg your pardon, sir?

JEKYLL takes the gladstone and puts the notebook he's been reading into it.

JEKYLL. I'm sorry. It's my father's notebooks. I never had a chance to read them in his lifetime.

POOLE. Well, I am sure they'll prove an inspiration, sir.

He picks up another bag. JEKYLL taps the portrait.

JEKYLL. In the hall. By the door to the dissecting room. Where that Caducci glass is now.

JEKYLL goes out with the gladstone.

Scene Four

Evening. A day or two later. JEKYLL's hall. 'A large, low-roofed, comfortable hall, paved with flags, warmed (after the fashion of a country house) by a bright open fire, and furnished with costly cabinets of oak'; in MR UTTERSON's opinion, 'the pleasantest room in London'. There is an exit on one side to the stairs and the front door, on the other a red baize door into JEKYLL's laboratory. Between is furniture and the portrait of JEKYLL's father, now hanging above the fireplace, at which UTTERSON

is presently looking. From offstage, the booming voice of
DR HASTIE LANYON.

LANYON *(off)*. Neuropathy.

JEKYLL *(off)*. Of course.

LANYON *(off)*. Phrenology?

JEKYLL *(off)*. Perhaps.

LANYON *(off)*. And naturalism?

JEKYLL *(off)*. Naturally.

LANYON *(off)*. Eugenicism.

JEKYLL *(off)*. Genics.

   Enter JEKYLL *and* LANYON. UTTERSON *sits.*

LANYON. What?

JEKYLL. I assume you mean, eugenics. Almost certainly.

LANYON. Oh, only 'almost'? Mesmerism.

JEKYLL. No.

LANYON. Hypnosis.

JEKYLL. Yes.

LANYON. Telepathy.

   JEKYLL *offering his cigar box to* LANYON, *who takes a
   cigar, and* UTTERSON, *who does not.*

JEKYLL. Well, I would need –

LANYON *(pressing his advantage)*. The occult? Astral bodies?
   Necromancy? Shamans?

JEKYLL. Lanyon. Really.

LANYON. Well, then. There you are.

   LANYON *sits.* POOLE e*nters with a tray of glasses and
   decanters.*

UTTERSON. So, gentlemen, if you'll allow me, as a mere layman,
   to summarize the arguments thus far . . .

JEKYLL. Or, as a lawyer, sum 'em up . . .

UTTERSON. . . . then, my good friend Dr Lanyon is of the
   opinion that the solution to our social ills lies in the
   amelioration of the physical environment, drains, sewage,
   overcrowding and the like, whereupon the material and mental
   and presumably the moral condition of the populace is
   miraculously transformed . . .

POOLE *proffers* LANYON *wine.*

POOLE. Port or claret, sir? It's Pichon-Longueville '65.

LANYON. Yes, thank you, Poole.

UTTERSON. Whereas my equally good friend Dr Jekyll thinks the mind's a kind of weaving mill, in which a thousand looms are constantly at labour, some effectively, some subject to malfunction –

POOLE. And for you, sir?

UTTERSON. Not tonight, Poole, no. I'll have a –

POOLE/UTTERSON – gin-and-water.

POOLE. Yes, of course.

UTTERSON. – of which eventually we'll understand the workings well enough to keep the lot of 'em in good repair.

JEKYLL. Well, not exactly –

UTTERSON. Then, amend.

JEKYLL. I merely said I was observing a dissection at the hospital, and marvelling at how much we know about the workings of our lungs and livers, and I was struck by the perception that one day we'll know as much about the warp and weft of human minds as we do about the mechanisms of the body.

LANYON. So, Utterson?

UTTERSON. Oh, as you would expect. Irredeemably old fashioned.

Taking his gin-and-water from POOLE.

Thanks, Poole.

LANYON. Well?

UTTERSON. My concern is that both of you remove responsibility for human actions from the actors. Blame brutishness on mutant brains, or drains. Whereas I must say I don't think the sewers are the only or the most important social problem in Soho. Or for that matter Whitechapel or Bethnal Green.

POOLE *gives* JEKYLL *his drink. We begin to hear knocking, faintly, from below stairs.* POOLE *goes, as:*

UTTERSON. But perhaps the topic is exhausted. Jekyll, you've been in the country.

JEKYLL. Yes. With my widowed sister. Who it seems has blossomed into what I take to be full-blown New Womanhood.

LANYON. I've never been quite sure what that means.

UTTERSON. As I understand it, free love, rational dress and neurasthenia.

JEKYLL. But not I assure you in this case.

LANYON. She was married to Charles Urquart, am I right?

JEKYLL. Correct.

UTTERSON. And that's presumably his portrait of your father.

JEKYLL. Yes.

LANYON. I hoped you've not sold that fine Caducci glass.

JEKYLL. No, no. I felt it wasn't – right, to have a mirror of that size in here.

A slightly edgy pause. To fill it:

LANYON. Yes, well, there's always something slightly chilling in a mirror. In medieval times, they say, when you saw death you saw an image of yourself.

UTTERSON. Which no doubt accounts for the old military legend of the mirrored shield. Did I hear someone at the door?

JEKYLL. Yes, I think you did. Poole will have seen to it.

LANYON. It's late for callers.

UTTERSON. Yes, it is.

JEKYLL. While it might be possible, of course, that like our brain our personalities are binary. That far from being one, we may possess two selves. A base half and a higher half. And that our lives are fundamentally a battleground on which they slug 'em out.

LANYON. Aha.

UTTERSON *goes to replenish his gin.*

UTTERSON. The question being – ?

JEKYLL. The question being, surely, what happens to the higher if the base is given sway. If a man *does* set his urges free . . . I suppose, he either tells the truth and shames the devil –

UTTERSON. Well, shame might certainly come into it –

POOLE *enters and hovers.*

JEKYLL. Or else puts on a false moustache and keeps it to himself –

UTTERSON. Well, that wouldn't salve his conscience, surely –

JEKYLL. Or else he sits on it.

UTTERSON. Well, he represses it. As so he should.

JEKYLL. And hopes it doesn't just – pop out.

LANYON *decides to help both* POOLE *and* JEKYLL *out.*

LANYON. Yes, Poole?

POOLE. Excuse me, sir. There's a young woman, sir. Who wants to speak with you.

JEKYLL. Oh, yes?

POOLE. She claims she's in your sister's service, sir.

JEKYLL. My sister? Ah. Ah, right. Well, I will see her shortly.

POOLE *goes out. There's a moment before* LANYON *decides to pick up the conversation where it left off.*

LANYON. Apparently, there's a neurological disorder they've identified in France. In essence, the sufferer cannot control the articulation of momentary emotion. So he feels anger, or frustration, or I suppose a more degraded urge, and it as you say pops out, involuntarily. The symptoms of this – singular condition are grimaces, tics, random salaciousness, compulsive mirroring and mockery. A delight in sheeny, glittering and spinning things. A kind of parody of the actions and reactions of an impulsive, wilful child.

UTTERSON. Which surely demonstrates why those not so afflicted should put childhood wilfulness behind them.

LANYON. Oh, you think so?

UTTERSON. Yes, I do. I think there are already pressures strong enough upon our weaker brethren, sucking them back towards the primitive. We need not look as far as Africa for proof the evolutionary road may run down as well as up. We may find it too in Stepney and Shoreditch. And it strikes me, gentlemen, that if indeed the cause of the debilitation of those places is a matter of dispute, then till it's settled we'd be best advised to set up barriers against their denizens, and man 'em. For there are too many borders but too tenuously in place, in these our gauzy times. Between the classes, and the races, and the sexes, and perhaps who knows within ourselves.

Pause.

For I am of a mind you see, that we live inside a little dish of light, surrounded by a black infinity of darkness. And it seems the darkness is forever clawing at the light, that our circle of security is shrinking, like a crumbling shoreline lapped by an insistent sea. For there are demons lurking out there in the darkness, gentlemen, and if we take a step beyond our gates, I tell you, they will have us.

LANYON. Demons.

UTTERSON. Yes.

Pause.

LANYON. Well, Henry, we must hope that they're not lurking round your door tonight. As it's time for me at least to pass through it and go home.

He stands.

JEKYLL. I'll ring for Poole.

LANYON. No need. I know where Poole keeps coats.

He's making to go but turns back.

As I know, Henry, that a man is not a manufactory, and that, Gabriel, the blackest ruffian in a Shoreditch rookery can choose the right, and if he lived in decency might even do so. And that what you saw of that poor drowned woman, Henry, was the least important part of her.

LANYON *goes out.*

UTTERSON. Ah. Dash it.

JEKYLL. Pardon?

UTTERSON. Lanyon. Think we strayed a little close to home. Quite inadvertently, in your case.

JEKYLL. Uh – how so?

Pause.

UTTERSON. Well, you're a doctor. You're discreet enough. There's something in the past.

JEKYLL. In Lanyon's?

UTTERSON. Yes. A long way back. He told me of it once, in general terms.

JEKYLL. I see.

UTTERSON. I didn't press him on specifics, naturally.

JEKYLL. No, naturally.

UTTERSON. As is my rule in matters of this kind.

JEKYLL. And a very good rule too.

UTTERSON. But as I recall, it sounded like the kind of youthful peccancy that looks a great deal worse in retrospect at forty-five than in actuality at two and twenty. As so of course it should.

JEKYLL. What do you mean?

UTTERSON. Oh, just the commonplace that what may be permissible at twenty is absurd at our age. Even yours.

Slight pause.

Well, there it is. The toe is trodden on, if toe it was.

Lightly.

I just wish he wouldn't call me Gabriel.

JEKYLL. It's not your name?

UTTERSON. Like you, I think, I take the view that when such a familiarity is absolutely unavoidable – sisters and so forth – a gentleman is best addressed not by his first but by his middle name.

LANYON *has entered, wearing his own coat, with* UTTERSON*'s coat, hat and cane.*

JEKYLL. Yes, I suppose that's right.

UTTERSON. What, that a gentleman –

JEKYLL. That what's forgivable at twenty is absurd at fifty.

UTTERSON. Jekyll. There is no 'suppose' about it.

LANYON. About what?

UTTERSON (*covering*). As I have frequent cause to tell my cousin. Who is proceeding rather more rapidly than he might wish to from the former to the latter.

LANYON. Your cousin?

UTTERSON. Richard Enfield.

LANYON. Oh. Perhaps you should invite him here one evening, Jekyll.

JEKYLL. Uh –

LANYON. Young blood. Might balance out the outmoded dogmas of the company.

UTTERSON *takes his coat from* LANYON.

UTTERSON. I trust outweighed by the pleasures of the Pichon-Longueville.

LANYON. I was in Trafalgar Square last evening. Surrounded by the people of the night. Lying shivering beneath their newspapers. And it struck me, just how close Trafalgar Square is to Pall Mall.

Enter POOLE.

POOLE. I'm sorry, sir, I didn't know . . .

LANYON. It's all right, Poole. Till the next time, gentlemen.

LANYON goes out with POOLE. *A moment between* UTTERSON *and* JEKYLL.

UTTERSON. Not just absurd. I'd say – downright dangerous.

He goes out.

JEKYLL. Yes. Goodnight.

POOLE re-enters.

POOLE. A agreeable occasion, sir?

JEKYLL. Yes. Yes, most satisfactory, thank you, Poole.

POOLE. So, you reached the right conclusion, sir.

JEKYLL. I'm sorry?

POOLE. On the question of the vintage.

JEKYLL. Oh, yes. Yes, absolutely.

He's making to go.

POOLE. And, your visitor?

JEKYLL. Of course. Uh, did she say -?

POOLE. She claims she's Mrs Urquart's parlour maid. In some distress. She says she's run away.

JEKYLL. What, from my sister?

POOLE. From her father, sir. If she's to be believed.

Slight pause.

JEKYLL. Then show her up, Poole.

POOLE. Beg your pardon, sir?

JEKYLL. Then show her up.

POOLE is a little shocked. He goes. JEKYLL, *alone, opens one of his father's notebooks.*

'For completion of the record, nonetheless . . . '

A moment. Then, a decision made, he tears the page from the notebook. He is about to toss it in the fire when POOLE *re-enters with* ANNIE, *clutching her overcoat.* JEKYLL *scrumples the paper and puts it into his pocket.*

POOLE. This is the person, sir.

JEKYLL. I thank you, Poole.

A moment. POOLE *goes out.*

Now, then. It's Annie?

ANNIE. Yes, sir.

JEKYLL. And I gather you've a problem.

ANNIE. Yes, you could say that, sir.

JEKYLL. With your father?

ANNIE. Yes, sir.

JEKYLL. So. Go on.

ANNIE. Well, it be as I tell Mr Poole, sir.

JEKYLL. Well, I'd like you to tell me.

Pause.

I mean, fathers do chastise their daughters.

ANNIE. True enough.

ANNIE *throws her coat over a chair, and pulls down her bodice, revealing livid weals and blisters on her neck.* JEKYLL *takes it in.*

JEKYLL. But this – but these are blisters. Like a scald or burn.

She nods.

From a – boiling liquid? or hot coals? If not . . .

ANNIE *puts her leg up on the arm of the chair and pulls up her skirt, revealing more crimson sores on her leg.*

. . . . a branding iron.

She nods again.

You could say . . . a fiend in human form.

She nods and looks away. She sees the portrait. She looks back at JEKYLL. *A moment. Then:*

So, does he give a reason?

ANNIE. If his beer's cloudy. If his bacon's salty. If the window be open and he do want her shut.

Pause.

And I has these distant relatives in – Hammersly? But I reckons they'd not follow it, and send me back. And I gets the address from the packages of books and that. And I be thinking – praying – as maybe you'll take me in.

Slight pause. JEKYLL *rings the bell.*

JEKYLL. I will have to write and tell my sister.

ANNIE. I do leave a note.

JEKYLL. Well, still. To say you're safe.

ANNIE. Just as long as he don't know sir, I don't care.

JEKYLL. And I think – in case you ever do look up your distant
relatives – I think it's 'Hammersmith'.

Enter POOLE.

Poole. Annie is staying with us, overnight at least.

POOLE. Yes, sir.

JEKYLL. We can discuss her future in the morning.

POOLE. Future, sir?

JEKYLL (*to* ANNIE). Do you have your box?

ANNIE. It be in the kitchen.

JEKYLL. Bring it up.

ANNIE *goes out.*

She can sleep in the back bedroom for tonight, and go up to the
quarters in the morning.

POOLE. Quarters, sir?

Slight pause.

JEKYLL. Poole, I mean to give this girl a situation in my household.

POOLE. If you say so, sir.

JEKYLL. She has been the victim of considerable mistreatment.

POOLE. Well, so we are invited to believe.

JEKYLL. Poole, you're a prig.

POOLE. I beg your pardon, sir.

JEKYLL. Oh, don't apologise. I'm envious.

Enter ANNIE *with her box.*

Ah, well done, Annie.

POOLE. Are you retiring now, sir?

JEKYLL. No. I think I'll work a little.

POOLE. Very good, sir.

JEKYLL. And in fact – Poole?

POOLE. Sir?

JEKYLL. You know that mirror? I've been thinking I should have
it in my room.

POOLE. The dissecting room?

JEKYLL. Yes. Annie, will you help Poole fetch the mirror for me?

ANNIE. Yes, sir. Certainly.

POOLE, *discomforted, goes out with* ANNIE. JEKYLL *goes and unlocks the red baize door. Then he takes the scrumpled paper from his pocket, opens it and reads.*

JEKYLL (*reads*). 'For completion of – etcetera . . . . I append the formula for both the initial metamorphosis – reputed to take full effect within a count of five-and-twenty – and for the 'opaque purple liquid' by which full reversion is supposedly achieved.'

POOLE *and* ANNIE *re-enter with the mirror, wrapped in a green cloth.* ANNIE *thinks they're going to take it through into the laboratory itself, but* POOLE *knows better.*

JEKYLL. Right, thank you. There.

As POOLE *and* ANNIE *lean the mirror up, the cloth slides off it.*

And now, Poole, a candle?

It's obviously for ANNIE.

POOLE. Yes, sir.

POOLE *goes out.*

ANNIE. Thank you, sir.

JEKYLL *is reaching to cover the mirror when he sees* ANNIE *looking at herself in it.* ANNIE *realises.*

ANNIE. Oh, I beg your pardon, sir.

JEKYLL. Don't worry. It's no matter.

Slight pause.

JEKYLL. So, then, why me? Why not your distant relatives in Hammersmith?

Pause.

ANNIE. Oh, sir.

JEKYLL. Go on.

ANNIE. Well . . . I suppose as how . . . it be as 'cos . . . I reckon you'd be game.

JEKYLL. That I'd be what?

ANNIE. I mean, like – like when you plays with Master Charles, sir, and Miss Lucy. 'Cos my experience is, sir, if you do play the child, then you still like has an understanding of how it be – to be one.

JEKYLL. Ah. I see.

ANNIE. And I'm a-reckoning right now I needs a party as'll see things from that point of view.

Pause.

JEKYLL. I hope so, Annie. Anyway.

Slight pause. He catches sight of himself and ANNIE *in the mirror.*

Apparently, in medieval times, when you saw death, you saw an image of yourself.

ANNIE. Be that a fact, sir?

Pause.

JEKYLL. Whilst for me, I think, the terror is to look and to see nothing. To be no more than a stain of breath upon the glass.

He breathes on the mirror and then wipes it. JEKYLL *and* ANNIE *look at each other.*

Sleep well.

JEKYLL carries the mirror into his laboratory. ANNIE looking after, thinking of looking in. But then JEKYLL re-appears, smiles, shuts the door, goes to the sideboard and picks up a bumper.

ANNIE. Does you want, be there anything as I can get you, sir?

JEKYLL. I'm sorry?

He realises what she's saying.

JEKYLL. No. No thank you, Annie. I have everything I need.

As he goes through into the laboratory, shutting and locking the door behind him, POOLE *enters with a candle.* ANNIE *turns to him.*

ANNIE. So tha's his bedroom?

POOLE. No. That's the dissecting room.

ANNIE. Say again?

POOLE. Before the master's time, it was a medical dissecting theatre. Where they cut dead bodies up for students.

ANNIE. Ooh. So what go on there now?

POOLE. It's where the master works. It's no concern of yours.

ANNIE. Be secret?

POOLE. No. Just private.

ANNIE. 'Cos my mistress – that's his sister – she do reckon as he's fascinated by the notion of those hidden faculties which lurk beyond the realms of human reason. Like hypnotics and tepelathy and such phenomenas.

POOLE. Well, does she now.

ANNIE *makes to take her candle. But* POOLE *nods to her box.*

This way.

ANNIE *picks up her box.*

And think yourself a most fortunate young person.

POOLE *leads* ANNIE *out. As she goes, she looks back at the red baize door. A fierce light comes up on the door. We can hear counting.*

JEKYLL. Twenty-five, twenty-four, twenty-three . . . . two . . . . twenty.

Pause.

Eighteen, seventeen, sixteen.

Pause.

Um . . . thirteen, twelve, eleven –

Suddenly something hits JEKYLL. *We can make out nothing for a few moments. Then, strangled.*

Seven . . .

A new voice: harsh, assured.

HYDE. Three. Two. One.

Scene Five

JEKYLL*'s Hall. Some weeks later.* POOLE *has admitted* UTTERSON, *who has not taken off his overcoat, nor parted with his hat and cane.*

UTTERSON. So, Poole. How long has this been going on?

POOLE. Oh, for several weeks, sir. Otherwise –

UTTERSON. You know of course your master has the right to give his keys to anyone he likes.

POOLE. Indeed so, sir. And I –

UTTERSON. And if your master walked in now and I told him what you've just told me –

POOLE. I'd lose my place, sir. There's no doubt about it.

UTTERSON. Then why the devil are you telling me?

Pause.

POOLE. Because, sir, of the nature of the man.

Slight pause. UTTERSON *places his cane on a sofa and sits on its arm.*

UTTERSON. Go on.

POOLE. Of something, something of him, in him.

UTTERSON (*impatient*). Yes?

POOLE. Of a – deformity. But not so much a physical deformity, as something missing. It's partly that he's . . . well, his way of speaking and demeanour is distasteful. But it's more than that. It's something I can't quite describe. But I can say, if I ever saw Satan's mark upon a face, it is that of my master's friend.

Pause.

UTTERSON. Poole, this is melodrama.

POOLE. You might think so, sir.

UTTERSON. Why should a man – a man as you describe, become a close associate and friend of Dr Jekyll?

POOLE. I have asked myself that question, sir.

UTTERSON. And come up with an answer?

POOLE. Only the obvious one, sir.

UTTERSON. Which is?

POOLE. That this man, this – gentleman, has some, some hold upon my master. Concerning some indiscretion from his past.

UTTERSON. Poole, that is not –

POOLE. But I know it's not for me to speculate.

UTTERSON. No, it is not, indeed. And this man – this gentleman – has become a frequent visitor?

POOLE. Oh, yes, sir.

UTTERSON. And does he dine here? Sleep here?

POOLE. No, he doesn't dine. Though he makes free enough with the master's cellar. And sometimes, he rests in the dissecting room. And I believe he keeps spare clothes in there.

UTTERSON. And he has keys to the outside doors.

POOLE. Yes, sir. The front door, naturally, and the back door, into the dissecting room.

UTTERSON. And does he have a name?

POOLE. Well, at first, sir, he was just my master's 'friend'.

UTTERSON. And now?

POOLE. We understand him to be Mr Hyde.

UTTERSON. And a Christian name?

POOLE. We have not had cause to know it.

UTTERSON. Well, I suppose there's not much reason why you should.

He stands.

So, then. You said that you had information for me. Now I stand informed.

POOLE. I hope I wasn't wrong to trouble you.

UTTERSON (*picking up his hat*). Well, what is done is done. And we need say no more about it. And who knows, some day I may meet this – misbegotten creature. And see if he's the penny dreadful you describe.

POOLE. Yes, sir.

Enter ANNIE, *with a candle. She looks startled by* UTTERSON.

UTTERSON. Hallo.

ANNIE. Oh, I'm sorry, sir. I be thinking you's the master, and you might be wanting summat.

UTTERSON. Well, I am not, and all I want to do is get back to my fireside and my bed. I'll see myself out, Poole.

POOLE. Yes, sir. Goodnight.

UTTERSON *has a second thought.*

UTTERSON. How old is Hyde?

POOLE. Oh, young, sir. Twenty, twenty-two. No more.

UTTERSON. I see.

Slight pause.

Well, that would argue against something from the past.

POOLE. Sir, may I take it then that you are of the view –

UTTERSON. No, Poole, I think you may take nothing of the kind.

He goes.

ANNIE. That be Mr Utterson.

POOLE. It is. He called round for a book.

ANNIE. And an'asking of that Mr Hyde?

POOLE. I've told you, twenty times –

ANNIE. 'Cos I've summat as I ought to tell him, if he do.

Pause.

POOLE. What's that?

ANNIE. Oh only as I thinks I has sight of the gentleman afore.

POOLE. What, Hyde? Before he came here?

ANNIE. Sure as sure be sure.

POOLE. So, when? And where?

ANNIE. Can't rightly say.

POOLE. 'Can't rightly say'. Indeed.

ANNIE *notices* UTTERSON's *stick on the sofa.*

ANNIE. Ooh, look. He left his stick.

POOLE. Who?

ANNIE. Mr Utterson.

POOLE. Ach. Why did you not say so first of all?

ANNIE. Only just noticed.

POOLE *takes the stick and hurries out after* UTTERSON.

ANNIE. Only just noticed.

POOLE *goes out.* ANNIE *alone, looks around. With the candle, she goes to the red baize door. She listens. Suddenly, the lock turns and the door opens.* ANNIE's *light blows out. A* MAN *is silhouetted in the doorway.* ANNIE *screams. The* MAN *comes into the room. It's* JEKYLL.

JEKYLL. Annie?

ANNIE. Ooh, I'm sorry, sir.

JEKYLL. What are you doing?

ANNIE. I be looking for a light, sir.

JEKYLL. Be you now.

ANNIE. I mean, I am looking for a light, sir.

JEKYLL *produces matches and lights* ANNIE's *candle.*

JEKYLL. Annie, did I hear a visitor?

ANNIE. Uh, yes, sir. Mr Utterson.

JEKYLL. Utterson? What for?

Pause.

ANNIE. I think he do come by for a book, sir.

JEKYLL. Ah. Ah, yes.

Pause.

ANNIE. Be there – Is there anything you're wanting, sir?

JEKYLL *going back to the laboratory.*

JEKYLL. No, no. You get to bed. I'm going to sleep down here.

Slight pause.

In fact, I might go out.

ANNIE (*quoting* CHARLES *and* LUCY*'s play*). Oh, 'by Jove, sir, 'tis a cruel night for such a one as you to be abroad'.

JEKYLL (*acknowledging the quotation, with a smile*). If not 'about'. Well, certainly. But even so.

JEKYLL *shuts the door behind him. The lock is turned. Re-enter* POOLE.

POOLE. Missed him. I'll have to have it sent round in the morning.

POOLE *puts down the cane.*

ANNIE. Well, certain, 'tis a cruel night –

POOLE. And you should be in bed.

POOLE *goes out.* ANNIE *alone. She thinks she hears something behind the door, and goes and listens.*

ANNIE. Twenty, nineteen, eighteen, seventeen . . . . ?

She listens a little longer. Then, reminded of the play, she starts to call LUCY*'s lines through the door.*

ANNIE. Oh, sir. Sir, do you want a box of lights? Or a stick of kindling?

'Cos I'll be honest, sir, I needs the ha'penny.

Ooh how I needs it, sir.

Enjoying herself.

So I would take it very kindly, sir, if you could see your way, sir. To the purchase of a stick of kindling. Or a tin of lampblack, sir. Or if not a box o' –

Suddenly, a small man in a cape and top hat darts through the door. He blows out ANNIE's *candle. He takes her in his arms and spins her round the room. It is* EDWARD HYDE.

HYDE. *One* two three *two* two three *three* two three one . . .

His rhythm changes.

And *one* and rest and rest and *two* and one and two and one and *rest* and rest . . .

ANNIE. Oh, sir. Oh, sir. I'm dizzy. Ooh, sir, I beg you, let me be.

A moment. Then HYDE *pulls back.*

Ooh, sir. You do make my head spin.

HYDE *smiles. He picks up* UTTERSON*'s cane.*

It's like – you know, the feeling, when you be on a high place, and you don't dare look down.

HYDE *moves in on* ANNIE, *using the tip of the cane to force her back against a wall; not violently, but teasingly.*

HYDE. I believe, the word you're looking for, is 'vertigo'.

Then, suddenly, he turns, leaves ANNIE, *and goes briskly out towards the night.*

Scene Six

London in winter. In an echo of the opening, UTTERSON *and* ENFIELD *appear, on either side of the stage.*

UTTERSON. And so?

ENFIELD. And so, when he reached her, the girl spoke to the man, offering him I think a box of lights. And then came the horrible part of the thing; for the man first smote her in the face, and then trampled calmly over the child's body, leaving her screaming on the ground.

Slight pause.

Not like a man, but like some damn Juggernaut. It sounds nothing to hear, but it was hellish to see.

Slight pause.

And I gave a view halloa, took to my heels and attempted to catch up with them.

UTTERSON. And so, the child?

ENFIELD. Not much the worse. Though naturally scared witless.

UTTERSON. And the door?

ENFIELD. Well, that was the strange thing. Because I could have sworn the man whipped out a key and went in through that door. But when I got there, and I hammered, there was no

sound and no reply. And the next day I came back, and tried
again, but could find no evidence of life, nor how that door
connects with any peopled habitation.

Scene Seven

JEKYLL's *Laboratory. There is a workbench with glasses
and jars; a sofa; bookshelves and glazed presses line the walls.
The full-length mirror in its ornate frame stands in a prominent
position. On one side is the red baize door, on the other a curtained window and the back door. Dressed for the night,* HYDE
*rushes through the back door, closing and locking it behind him.
He crows:*

HYDE. Lights! Box of lights! Fine cotton thread! Best kindling!
Lampblack! Lights! Lights! Li-i-i-i-ights!

High on his violence, HYDE *strides, hops, marches and dances
round the room, singing loudly.*

HYDE. Ring-a-ring-a-*roses.*
A pocket full-a-*posies.*
A-tishoo a-tishoo
All fall down.

He changes song and step.

Gi' a body meet a body
Coming through the rye.
Gi'a body, kiss a body
Need a –

HYDE *is interrupted by knocking and calls from* ENFIELD *at
the back door.* HYDE *freezes.*

ENFIELD (*calls*). Is anyone there? Open up! Open up, I say!

HYDE *remains frozen.*

Is anybody there?

A pause. Then HYDE, *in an elaborate whisper.*

HYDE. Give a body, kiss a body,
Need a body cry.

We hear the cry of the MATCHGIRL.

MATCHGIRL. Help! Please help!

ENFIELD. All right!

HYDE *listens to* ENFIELD's *departing footsteps. Then he goes
to the red baize door, listens, unlocks and quickly opens it. He*

brings in a tray of food on a round silver tray that has been left there, locking the door behind.

Oh well. The wee queen's set us out a banquet here.

He takes food from the tray and shovels it into his mouth.

Cold mutton. Pickle. Glass of hock. A fine hot toasted bun.

He knocks back the hock. At the workbench, he begins to make the purple liquid that will transform him back into JEKYLL, *in a graduated glass. As he does so, he sings, again in a whisper.*

Is that Mr Reilly, can anyone tell;
Is that Mr Reilly that owns the hotel?
Well if that's Mr Reilly they speak of so highly:
Upon me soul Reilly, you're doing quite well.

He adds a final ingredient.

Upon me soul, Reilly, you're doing quite well!

On the bench is JEKYLL's *journal. It catches* HYDE's *eye.*

Oho. What have we here. Some class of diary or journal?

He turns back to the beginning and reads. Of course, HYDE *knows what* JEKYLL *has written, but he affects to be reading it for the first time, as a schoolmaster might read out a schoolchild's essay as if on first aquaintance, for sarcastic rhetorical effect.*

HYDE. 'I was born in the year 1836 to a large fortune, endowed besides with excellent parts, inclined by nature to industry, fond of the approbation of my fellows and thus as might have been supposed with every guarantee of an honourable and distinguished future.' So, what's this, a novel?

HYDE *flips through the pages and reads on:*

'But then through my experiments I began to perceive more deeply than it has ever yet been stated' – *weel* – 'the trembling immateriality, the mist-like transcience' – weel, *phew* – 'of this seemingly so solid frame . . . ' Oh, I see. It's a *tract.*

He turns the pages and reads on:

'The indulgences that I made haste to satisfy were to say the least "undignified" . . . Into the details of the infamy at which I thus connived I have no design of entering' – oh, go on . . .

HYDE *turns a page and reads on:*

'Men have before hired bravoes to transact their crimes; I was the first that ever did so for his pleasures. I was the first that could plod piously in the public eye, then like a schoolboy, strip off these lendings and spring headlong into a sea of liberty.' Well, *yeah* . . . 'And while initially I found myself plunged into a kind of wonder, aghast yet awed before the acts of Edward Hyde . . . ' oh, please . . . 'increasingly I came to understand that his activities had taken independent life, that his infamies were not of my making or desiring but his own.'

Slight pause. A note of concern:

Oh, now I get it. It's a legal deposition. It's your *defence*.

He reads on:

'That far from being an embodiment of my own sensuality unstayed, the lack of the constraining hand of culture turned my nature into something other than itself.'

HYDE *looks up ruminatively.*

Och, is that so.

HYDE *reads on:*

'Indeed, increasingly I came to find its pleasures, even its enormities, a laughable distortion of my own indulgences; increasingly I saw in them a vulgar boorishness which placed my predilections in proportion and threw my own respectability into relief'.

Pause.

I see.

He knocks back the purple liquid. He looks at his pocket watch. He is taking the glass back to the tray when he turns back to check a point.

'A laughable distortion'. And 'plac*ed*'. And 'thr*ew*'.

He goes and puts the glass on the tray, picking it up to take it to the door.

Well, well.

In a sudden burst of fury, he throws the tray at the wall.

So that's it, eh?

HYDE *runs back to the book, takes a pen, and scrawls violently across the page. As he does so, the pangs of transformation hit him.*

'Boorishness'. 'Vulgar'. 'My respectability . . . . into relief . . . '

HYDE *flings the book to the floor in his last gesture before changing into* JEKYLL. *The older man stands before us. He takes his watch from his pocket and looks at it. In slight surprise:*

JEKYLL. Twenty-six seconds.

He looks at the smashed glass on the floor. He hears ANNIE *call from outside, beyond the red baize door.*

ANNIE (*calls*). Sir? Be all well with you?

JEKYLL *calls back, as he picks up the book:*

JEKYLL. Yes, thank you, Annie! Just a mishap. All 'be very well'.

With trepidation, JEKYLL *opens the book to read* HYDE'*s scrawling.*

'It's you. It's you. I'm you.'

HENRY JEKYLL *closes his eyes.*

Scene Eight

JEKYLL'*s hall. Five days later.* UTTERSON, LANYON *and* ENFIELD *have come round for dinner.* POOLE *and* ANNIE *are in attendance. The eight o'clock chime begins.* UTTERSON *looks at his watch. The chime concludes.*

LANYON. So, sir, I understand you are of a perambulatory persuasion.

ENFIELD. Uh – I'm sorry?

UTTERSON. Sunday walks.

ENFIELD. Oh, yes.

Slight pause.

Indeed, last Sunday, not too far from –

UTTERSON (*interrupting*). Poole. He did remember?

POOLE. Oh, yes, sir. He gave his usual instructions, for the wine and so forth.

LANYON. And he was aware, we had an extra guest?

POOLE. Oh, yes. I know he had a number of appointments.

UTTERSON. And he's not been back?

POOLE. Not as far as I'm aware, sir, no.

Pause. UTTERSON *glances at the laboratory door.*

UTTERSON. But of course – there is a back door.

LANYON. It is possible to be so immersed in work one loses track of time.

UTTERSON. To a degree.

POOLE. I have – been knocking, sir.

UTTERSON. Well, let's try once again.

He goes to the laboratory door and raps sharply on it.

Hallo, there, Jekyll? Jekyll!

Pause. He turns, shrugs, and returns.

Well, there it is, he obviously forgot.

ENFIELD. I don't suppose, there's nothing could have happened . . .

UTTERSON. No, I'm sure it's nothing. He has been delayed. The calls of business.

LANYON *looks at his watch.*

LANYON. Nonetheless . . .

POOLE. Sir, there is – the dinner is prepared . . . .

UTTERSON. No, I think that we'll be off. Unless, uh, Lanyon . . .

LANYON. No, in fact, there's some political affair I had to turn down for this evening. I may slope along to that.

POOLE *nods to* ANNIE, *who goes out for coats.*

UTTERSON. Well, I wish you joy of it.

LANYON *picks up that* UTTERSON *wants to stay a moment.* ENFIELD *doesn't.*

LANYON. I thankee. Till the next time – Utterson.

LANYON *goes out. When he's gone.*

UTTERSON. Well, I must apologise.

ENFIELD. No matter.

Slight pause. Gesturing to the red baize door.

So this is – where he works?

UTTERSON. Dr Jekyll is a gentleman of considerable private means.

ENFIELD. No, I meant – this is his working room.

Slight pause. UTTERSON *doesn't want this to go any further now.*

UTTERSON. It is.

ENFIELD*'s trying to work out the geography of the house.*

ENFIELD. And that's the front door, leading to the square –

UTTERSON. That's right. Ten minutes to Pall Mall. I trust that this won't prove an entirely wasted evening.

ENFIELD *realises* UTTERSON *wants him to leave.*

ENFIELD. No. Well, perhaps the next time. Goodnight, Utterson.

ENFIELD *goes out.*

UTTERSON. Poole, do you have any reason for concern about your master's whereabouts tonight?

POOLE. No, sir. Well, not beyond the matter we discussed.

UTTERSON. I see.

He makes a decision. He takes out a letter in an envelope.

UTTERSON. Poole, this is a letter from your master.

POOLE. Yes, sir, I recognise it.

UTTERSON. So, you posted it?

POOLE. Well, certainly, I remember sending it out to the evening post.

UTTERSON. And you received it from his hand?

Slight pause.

POOLE. No, sir.

UTTERSON. From whose, then?

POOLE. From Annie, sir, the parlour maid. There'd been an accident, with a tray of crockery. She'd been called to the dissecting room to clear it up.

UTTERSON. I'd like a word with her.

POOLE. Of course.

POOLE *goes out, returning with* ANNIE, *who carries* UTTERSON's *coat, hat and cane.*

ANNIE. Ooh, beg pardon, sir, I be waiting in the hallway with your things.

UTTERSON. Now, Annie, did your master give you this? About two weeks ago?

He shows ANNIE *the letter.*

ANNIE. Yes, sir.

UTTERSON. And he gave it you himself?

ANNIE. That's right. In fact, I sees him finishing it off, and then he stuffs it in that envelope and seals it down.

UTTERSON. I see.

Slight pause.

Well, there's no arguing with that.

ANNIE. So glad to be of service sir.

UTTERSON *puts down the letter to take his coat, hat and cane.*

UTTERSON. Oh, by the by, Poole, you haven't traced that other cane of mine?

POOLE. No, sir. I can't think where . . .

UTTERSON (*to* ANNIE). And I don't suppose you saw an errant walking stick, in the dissecting room?

ANNIE. No, sir. But then master don't like people poking round in there. I just pops in to sweep up plates and a glass he drops and I keep my eye on that.

UTTERSON. Yes, very right. Well, I've no doubt it'll show up in due course. I'll see myself out, Poole.

He picks up the letter and makes to go.

POOLE. Um, sir . . .

UTTERSON. Yes, what?

POOLE. Sir, may I ask, if the burden of this letter –

UTTERSON. No, you may not, Poole. Goodnight.

He goes out. ANNIE *is secretly pleased with* POOLE'*s discomfort.*

POOLE. Well, I'd best tell cook what's happened.

ANNIE. Yes, you'd best.

POOLE. And you can see the master's bedroom fire's kept up. Who knows when he'll be back.

ANNIE. That's true enough.

POOLE *looks at* ANNIE *and goes out.* ANNIE *smiles. She takes a candle to go upstairs. As she passes the red baize door, she hears something. She puts her ear to the door.*

ANNIE. Thirteen, twelve, eleven, ten . . . six, five . . .

Pause.

So it must be four.

Slight pause.

Whatever 'tis.

She listens again. Nothing else is going to happen. She's leaving when she hears the key turn in the lock of the red baize door. She turns. The door slowly swings open. ANNIE *waits a moment, then walks over and goes through.*

Scene Nine

JEKYLL's *laboratory.* ANNIE *appears. She – and we – can't immediately see anyone in the shadows. She looks round the room. She sees the mirror and goes and looks at herself in it with evident pleasure. Suddenly, she and we see* HYDE.

ANNIE. Uh – beg pardon sir. I do think – I do think be Dr Jekyll.

HYDE. Well, do ye now.

HYDE *closes and locks the red baize door. Suddenly, he moves in on* ANNIE, *pinning her up against the mirror, and kissing her full on the mouth. He pulls back for a moment.*

Dinya fret, hen. It be just the two of us.

Blackout.

ACT TWO

Scene Ten

JEKYLL*'s laboratory. Two months later.* JEKYLL *is reading his notebook. His father's wine-glass stands on the workbench beside him. It is full.*

JEKYLL. Accordingly. 'Accordingly, I resolved that for all his dry restraint, I preferred the elderly and discontented doctor, surrounded by friends and cherishing honest hopes; and bade farewell to the liberty, the comparative youth, the light step and leaping pulse, that I had enjoyed in the disguise of Hyde. True to my determination, I led a life of such severity in words and works as I had never before attained to, and enjoyed the compensations of an approving conscience.'

He looks at the glass. A pause.

But.

Breathing deeply, he drinks the draught.

'But time began at last to obliterate the freshness of my alarm. The praises of conscience began to grow into a thing of habit. I began to be tortured . . . with those dormant throes and longings . . . I had thought . . . '

The convulsions hit him.

' – and so at last . . . '

HYDE *emerges from* JEKYLL. *Looking at the pocket watch.*

HYDE. Eight. Seven. Six.

He goes and looks in the mirror.

You're me.

Scene Eleven

London in winter. The same night. Above, a MAID *in a nightshirt with a rug round her shoulders stands looking out of a high window.* ENFIELD *and* UTTERSON *appear.*

ENFIELD. While in the early months of winter, London was startled by a crime of singular ferocity,

MAID. So, sir, it went this way.

UTTERSON. Rendered all the more notable by the high position of the victim.

MAID. I was in my room, and I was standing on my box, and looking at the stars . . .

ENFIELD. The details,

UTTERSON. Which were few,

ENFIELD. Came from the evidence of a maid-servant,

MAID. . . . as I likes to do of a clear night and I can't get up there 'less I stands on something 'cos the window's awful high.

UTTERSON. whose attic bedroom overlooked the river,

MAID. And at first I don't see nothing but the stars, and all I hear's the lapping of the river . . .

ENFIELD. Lit brilliantly by the full moon.

ENFIELD *and* UTTERSON *withdraw.*

MAID. And I'll be straight, sir, I hardly ever feels more kindly or at peace with things, as how the stars and moons and that are s'posed to make you feel. And then I hears the tap tap of a footfall and there's an old man with white hair and stick. And then I hears a second tapping, and I has to stand on tip-toe, so as I can see the other one.

And by now dim light is coming up on SIR DANVERS CAREW, *on the one side of the stage, and* MR HYDE *on the other. They are both wrapped up well and carry sticks.*

CAREW. Good evening.

HYDE. Pardon?

CAREW. Uh – good evening.

HYDE. Can I help you?

CAREW. No. No, I don't think so, thank you.

HYDE. Oh.

CAREW *makes to go.*

Well maybe you could help me.

CAREW. Uh – I beg your pardon?

HYDE (*taking out a cigar*). Like – if you had a light?

CAREW *smiles.*

CAREW. I'm sorry, no.

HYDE. No light.

CAREW. No. No, I'm sorry.

HYDE. And you're sure that I can't help you.

CAREW. Thank you, really. No.

> CAREW *makes to go. He turns back.*

Unless . . .

> HYDE *looks quizzically at* CAREW.

I am looking for a hansom. I am told there is a hansom stand nearby.

HYDE. Oh, a *hansom stand.*

CAREW. That's – yes.

HYDE. You're lost?

CAREW. No. I am not lost. And I will find a cabstand. Thank you.

HYDE. Thank you sir.

> HYDE *blocks* CAREW*'s path.*

CAREW. I beg your pardon?

HYDE. Do you no say 'sir' when you thank a party?

> CAREW *attempts to pass* HYDE, *who gives a little shuffle. It is not absolutely clear to* CAREW *that* HYDE *is barring him.*

Do you no say 'thank you, sir'?

> *Again* CAREW *attempts to get round* HYDE *but finds himself prevented.*

I mean, if you gave me a light, I would say 'thank you sir'. But you don't have one.

CAREW. No.

HYDE. So I'll have to use my own.

> HYDE *lights his cigar as* CAREW *tries to hurry out. But* HYDE *overtakes him.*

So may I ask your name sir?

CAREW. Look, I'm sorry, it is very late.

HYDE. Too late for courtesy it seems.

CAREW. My name sir is Carew. And now –

HYDE. Carew.

CAREW. That's right. Now, really –

HYDE. Surely not – Carew, Sir Danvers. The noted backbench
member?

CAREW. Yes.

HYDE. The parliamentarian extraordinaire?

CAREW. Well, there are those who might contest –

HYDE. Oh, the privilege. The honour. To have met Sir Danvers.
To have him pay the briefest moment's heed to me.

Pause.

Sir Danvers. Sir. The cabstand lies that way.

CAREW *a slight bow.*

CAREW. I thank you kindly – sir.

CAREW *moves.* HYDE *hits* CAREW *on the back of his head
with his stick.*

Uh – wha' –

HYDE. But it seems your stroll is interrupted.

HYDE *hits* CAREW *again.*

CAREW. Sir – sir, please –

HYDE. Oh, sir. Sir, *now.*

HYDE *hits* CAREW.

CAREW. What cause have I –

HYDE. From the man who thinks he's something to the man he
thinks is nothing –

CAREW. Uh, I never said –

HYDE *crushing* CAREW's *windpipe with the stick.*

HYDE. Who does he think he is now?

CAREW *choking to death.*

'Cos I'd say now as things were o'er much the other way about.

CAREW *is still.* HYDE *is playing with his body like a puppet.*

Would you no say? Sir Danvers? Sir? That the boot is on the
other foot?

Holding the head up and asking it.

Who – are – *you* – now?

The MAID *lights a match.*

MAID. Help! Police! Help! Murder! Help!

HYDE *runs out, leaving the stick behind him.*

Scene Twelve

JEKYLL*'s Laboratory.* HYDE *rushes in, slamming and locking the back door behind him. He runs quickly to his workbench to prepare a dose of the antidote draught that will change him back. As he works he mumbles, desperately:*

HYDE. O Lord look down on me a miserable sinner . . . and from the infinity of thy endless grace pour down thy cooling draughts of mercy on my wretched head . . .

He takes the draught.

. . . confessing that the world is set in firm and final struggle between God and evil for the eternal mastery of all creation . . .

He is hit by the effects of the draught.

Thirteen, fourteen . . . and owning that in thy sight all our righteousness is but as filthy rags . . . twenty-one . . .

He is turning into JEKYLL.

O Lord, strike not my number from the Book of Life, and pluck me as a brand from out the burning . . . twenty-seven – twenty-nine.

JEKYLL *has emerged from* HYDE. *He closes his eyes in thanksgiving.*

JEKYLL. So that . . . I may be named forever in the association of the perfect and the just.

JEKYLL *hears a knocking in the house. He looks round. He begins to take off* HYDE*'s jacket.*

Scene Thirteen

JEKYLL*'s Hall. The knocking continues. Eventually* ANNIE *appears, in nightclothes. She is clearly unwell. She admits* UTTERSON.

UTTERSON. Annie.

ANNIE. Mr Utterson.

UTTERSON. Is your master in?

ANNIE. I don't rightly know sir. He baint in when I goes to bed.

UTTERSON. Annie, are you all right?

Pause.

ANNIE. Not so you'd notice, if I be honest, sir. But I think it be
the partridge pie as we has on Tuesday. They be a danger to a
body, there's no question, be meat pies.

UTTERSON. Yes. There's truth in that.

Enter JEKYLL *in his dressing gown from the laboratory.*

JEKYLL. Utterson?

UTTERSON. Jekyll.

JEKYLL *nods to* ANNIE, *who goes.*

JEKYLL. I'm sorry. I was sleeping in the lab.

UTTERSON. Jekyll, there's dreadful news. Sir Danvers Carew has
been murdered.

JEKYLL. What, the MP?

UTTERSON. That's right.

JEKYLL. But where, and how?

UTTERSON. He was walking by the river. Where he was met by a
young man. Who battered him to death.

JEKYLL. How appalling.

UTTERSON. A short young man. Of singularly primitive appearance.

JEKYLL. And the weapon?

UTTERSON. Was my walking-stick. Or rather, was a walking
stick of mine.

Pause.

JEKYLL. You're sure of this?

UTTERSON. I am.

JEKYLL. And the police know?

UTTERSON. Certainly. My initials are engraved on it. And he –
Sir Danvers, had a letter from my office in his pocket.

JEKYLL. And are you suspected?

UTTERSON. Naturally. Although I told them it was a walking
stick I had mislaid some weeks ago. Almost certainly, I said, in
the house of a close friend.

JEKYLL *says nothing.*

There is no doubt about it, surely? That the murderer is your friend Hyde? The one to whom you have opened up your house? And who has already been observed in acts of senseless violence?

JEKYLL. What do you mean?

UTTERSON. I mean – I have a distant cousin, by the name of Enfield. Who witnessed – an attack, by Hyde, upon some urchin, outside your back door. As I understand it, also, with that cane of mine.

JEKYLL. And you told them? Where you thought you'd left it?

UTTERSON. Where I did leave it. No, I said I wanted to be sure. Before I involved a gentleman in such a scandal. And they gave me until nine.

Pause.

JEKYLL. Well, you must tell them.

UTTERSON. And when they call on you?

JEKYLL. I will confirm the cane was in my house but I am unaware of how it was purloined. As are my staff.

UTTERSON. But you suspect . . .

JEKYLL. That I have been shamefully betrayed. By a man in whom I placed my trust. And who has repaid my generosity in heinous fashion.

UTTERSON. And do you know where this man is?

Slight pause.

JEKYLL. No I do not.

UTTERSON. Or seen him recently? Say, in the last three days?

JEKYLL. I have not seen him face to face.

UTTERSON. And may I take it that whatever bond may tie you, or whatever hold he has on you, you are no longer his protector?

JEKYLL. Oh, Utterson, you think –

UTTERSON. I don't know what to think. So let me ask it plainly. Jekyll, you've not been mad enough to hide this fellow?

Pause.

Because if you have, then for God's sake –

JEKYLL. No. No, I have not hidden Mr Hyde. And wherever he may be, I shall not see his face again. For I have cut him off and done with him. And if there was ever – any bond, or hold, then it is severed now. And I am – so much the better man for it.

Pause.

UTTERSON. You have had a fine escape.

JEKYLL. I can expect the officers a little after nine?

UTTERSON. I am afraid so, yes.

JEKYLL. An hour. Will you take some breakfast?

UTTERSON. No. No, thank you.

JEKYLL. It would only take a moment. I can call the maid.

UTTERSON. No, let the poor girl be.

JEKYLL. Poor girl?

UTTERSON. She was white as chalk just now. And she'd obviously been vomiting. Apparently, a less than wholesome slice of Tuesday's partridge pie.

JEKYLL. I see.

UTTERSON. Look, Jekyll –

JEKYLL. Look, Utterson –

Polite waving on.

UTTERSON. Do go –

JEKYLL. No, please –

JEKYLL *wins.*

UTTERSON. Well, you'd expect this matter to come up. In October, I received a letter written in your hand.

JEKYLL. You did.

UTTERSON. It requested me to draw up a power of attorney in the name of –

JEKYLL. Yes.

UTTERSON. Which naturally I did. Albeit with extreme reluctance.

JEKYLL. Yes.

UTTERSON. So may I now assume that this instruction is no longer – well, applicable?

JEKYLL. That's correct.

UTTERSON. And I can burn the letter?

JEKYLL. Yes. Oh, please, please, yes.

Slight pause.

UTTERSON. Thank God.

Slight pause.

But, forgive me. You were going to say.

JEKYLL. I was?

UTTERSON. I thought I interrupted you.

Slight pause.

JEKYLL. Oh, yes. Well, no.

Slight pause.

No the matter is no longer – as you say, applicable.

UTTERSON. Look, Jekyll. You know this is a rancid sort of business. So why not, when you've seen the police, and shown your face around a week or two . . . Why not take a few days out of town. Go and see your sister in the country, breathe in some fresh air. And put it all behind you.

JEKYLL. Yes. Perhaps I will.

Slight pause.

But Utterson –

UTTERSON. Not one more syllable. Just thank your star.

He goes out. Pause. Then JEKYLL *rings his bell.* POOLE *appears.*

POOLE. I'm sorry, sir. I didn't realise you'd risen.

JEKYLL. It's all right. Poole, some policemen will be here within the hour.

Slight pause.

POOLE. May I ask in what connection, sir?

JEKYLL. In connection with – with Mr Hyde.

POOLE. Is that so, sir?

JEKYLL. Who from now on, if he shows his face – is to be denied all access to this house. Indeed, the police are to be called at once. And I would like the back door of my room securely bolted.

POOLE. I will have it done this morning, sir.

POOLE *makes to go.*

JEKYLL. Oh, Poole. How long has Annie Loder been unwell?

POOLE. She has been a little nauseous for some days. But didn't want to trouble you.

JEKYLL. Well, she has failed in that endeavour. Call her, please.

POOLE. Yes, sir.

POOLE goes out. JEKYLL looks at his father's portrait.
POOLE returns with ANNIE.

JEKYLL. Annie, I'm most distressed to hear you are unwell.

ANNIE. Oh, sir. It be – it's nothing, honest.

JEKYLL. After all, I am a doctor.

ANNIE. Yes, I knows that, sir, but I din't want to be no bother.

JEKYLL. And how long have you felt like this?

ANNIE. Uh . . .

JEKYLL. Poole, when did we last have game pie in this house?

POOLE. I don't remember, sir. Certainly not since you told cook
  that the consumption of dead wildfowl was a corruption to the
  constitution if not an actual affront to decency.

Slight pause.

JEKYLL. Yes, I thought so. Thank you, Poole.

POOLE takes this to mean dismissal. He goes.

JEKYLL. So how long have you known?

ANNIE. Known what?

JEKYLL. Your state.

ANNIE. My state?

JEKYLL. Or if you prefer, 'condition'.

ANNIE. I don't rightly get your meaning sir.

JEKYLL. So when did you last show?

Heavily sarcastic.

'Ooh, sir, and I says a word to Mrs Urquart, like I don't know
what he'd do to me.'

ANNIE. It's not true sir.

JEKYLL. Of course not. It was partridge pie.

ANNIE. Sir, I means the veal pie. As we has last Wednes-

JEKYLL. What interests me you see is whether you were in this
  state when you came into my house, on the pretext that I was so
  transparently – I think your word was 'game'.

ANNIE. Sir –

JEKYLL. You will leave this house this instant. You will not
  expect a character and you will not receive one. Now, send
  Poole to me.

He turns, goes to the red baize door. He is fumbling for his keys. ANNIE *decides to have one last go.*

ANNIE. Please, sir.

JEKYLL. Yes, what?

ANNIE. Would you like your fire made up, sir?

JEKYLL. No. No, I would not.

He opens the door.

ANNIE. Or your breakfast bringing up, sir.

JEKYLL. No.

ANNIE. Or anything.

JEKYLL *is turning to berate* ANNIE *when she speaks, quickly but not blurted, to him.*

'Cos sir you're quite right, obviously, I got myself in trouble and be doubtless very sinful. But I weren't in that state when I first came here. And all I tells you of my father and the way he treats me, all that be true.

Slight pause.

And all right I tells a lie just now but I didn't tell no lie afore and I bet you'd do the same in my place. And let's be honest, 'cos it don't need that much reckoning, you throw me out and it be living on the streets or dying there.

JEKYLL. Come come –

ANNIE. And I'm sorry if I called you game but be how you strikes me at the time. And I can't see how I bear the blame of that. In fact, I won't bear it, when your friend Mr Hyde –

JEKYLL. Be silent. You will not add – slander to your other malefactions.

JEKYLL *does not look at* ANNIE. *He goes to the bell and pulls it.* ANNIE *changes tack.*

ANNIE. 'Cos to be honest sir –

JEKYLL. Honest!

ANNIE. I needs the ha'penny.

JEKYLL *chooses not to recognise the quotation from the play.*

JEKYLL. The what?

ANNIE. I needs – I need – the ha'penny.

JEKYLL. The ha'penny?

POOLE *enters.*

POOLE. Sir?

JEKYLL. Poole. Ann and I have had a conversation.

POOLE. Yes, sir?

JEKYLL. And it appears you were correct in your first suspicion of her character.

POOLE. I was, sir?

JEKYLL. She has in short abused my generosity and your considerable indulgence. She will be out of here by nine o'clock. If she reappears today or any other day, you will have her thrown in gaol for vagrancy. In short, she is now cut off from us and – and we have done with her.

Slight pause.

Is that all clear?

POOLE. Yes. Yes of course, sir.

JEKYLL. And you have issued my instructions on the bolting of the door?

POOLE. I have – I will have it set in train at once, sir.

JEKYLL. Oh, and Poole. I would like my father's portrait hung in the dissecting room.

POOLE. And, uh, the mirror, sir?

JEKYLL. You may put it where you like. I have no further need of it.

POOLE. Yes, sir.

ANNIE *looking fixedly at* JEKYLL, *as he walks to the door of his laboratory.*

JEKYLL. Of course, you could not be to blame. You were doubtless overcome with vertigo.

He goes into the laboratory and shuts the door.

POOLE. You heard the master.

ANNIE. Yes I did.

POOLE. I've never seen him in this way before.

ANNIE. Oh, no?

POOLE. But still. You heard his or-

ANNIE. He knows the words he uses without telling.

POOLE. Who knows whose words?

ANNIE. Dr Jekyll. Mr Hyde. Be as if he thinks and master speaks. Be as if he's got inside the master's mind.

POOLE *looks at* ANNIE.

POOLE. No, I've never seen the doctor in this way.

POOLE *goes out, as lights fade.*

Scene Fourteen

The laboratory. JEKYLL *leans against the baize door, breathing deeply. After a moment, he goes and opens his notebook. He writes:*

JEKYLL. 'The problem of my conduct was thus solved. Hyde was henceforth impossible. I was now confined to the better part of my existence. And I rejoiced in it.'

He closes the book.

Like a stain of breath upon the glass.

He looks in the mirror at himself.

How could you be me. Look at what I am.

Scene Fifteen

Winter in the country. We are in the drawing room of KATHERINE'*s house on a Sunday afternoon shortly after Christmas. The curtains are closed; a roaring fire burns in the grate, wine is set out on a side table. Decorations are still up.* KATHERINE *is there. There is a tap on the window. She looks round. Another tap. She goes and opens the curtains. Two white, ghostly* FACES *peer in. They belong to* CHARLES *and* LUCY.

KATHERINE. Oh, Lucy. Charles. It's you.

KATHERINE *admits* CHARLES *and* LUCY.

CHARLES. O kind mistress, pardon us for this intrusion . . .

KATHERINE. Oh Charles, your *boots* . . .

LUCY. But we be a pair of humble ploughboys, all muddy and mired . . .

CHARLES *closing the window.*

KATHERINE. Which is why one does not wear them in the parlour.

CHARLES. – and a catching sight of your nice warm fire . . .

LUCY. – and a-hearing talk of the pies and cakes and suchlike noted in these parts . . .

KATHERINE. One can assume the expedition was successful?

CHARLES. It was *wonderful*.

LUCY. You can skate right down to Jenkin's Mill.

CHARLES. Though Lucy didn't.

LUCY. Quite.

KATHERINE. I am delighted. Now –

LUCY. And maybe Uncle Henry will come out tomorrow.

Slight pause.

KATHERINE. We will have to see.

CHARLES. A phrase well-known to mean, 'most likely not'.

KATHERINE. A phrase in this case meaning that it's up to Uncle Henry.

And in fact JEKYLL *has entered.*

JEKYLL. What is up to Uncle Henry?

KATHERINE. Whether tomorrow you go skating with the children.

LUCY. Oh Uncle Henry, do please say you will.

CHARLES. It was wonderful today.

The CHILDREN *grab* JEKYLL'*s legs.*

LUCY. You can go for miles.

CHARLES. Much further than last year.

LUCY. And you've been here a whole day and you haven't played a single –

JEKYLL (*breaking free*). Katherine, is it usual, for your children to be out at such an hour?

Slight pause.

And on a Sunday?

KATHERINE. It is – they should certainly have had their tea.

Slight pause.

Off, now.

LUCY. But he will, tomorrow, you'll come skating, won't you, uncle?

JEKYLL. Well, we shall –

CHARLES. And mama said in the morning she would take our photograph, that's you and me and Lucy, and she has been looking forward to it ever so –

JEKYLL. Well, we shall have –

LUCY. Oh and please, dear uncle, don't say 'we shall have to see' because it's a phrase *well* known to mean –

KATHERINE. Now, Lucy, please. And Charles, the both of you. What will your uncle think of us.

LUCY. Hm. Sorry.

She goes and kisses JEKYLL.

Goodnight, then, Uncle Henry.

JEKYLL. Goodnight Lucy.

LUCY *goes out.*

Goodnight Charles.

CHARLES. Goodnight.

He is making to go.

JEKYLL. Goodnight, sir.

CHARLES *looks back at* JEKYLL.

CHARLES. Pardon?

JEKYLL. Do you not say, 'goodnight, sir'?

CHARLES (*quizzically*). Goodnight, sir.

He goes out.

KATHERINE. Henry, I should say, in this house, it is not our custom to observe too many strict formalities.

JEKYLL. Or common courtesies, it seems.

Pause.

KATHERINE. They do – enjoy your company.

JEKYLL. Then all the more –

KATHERINE. Or, did.

Pause. KATHERINE *goes to the wine.*

Would you like some wine?

JEKYLL. No, thank you.

KATHERINE. Oh, I'm sorry, I'd forgotten. Sunday.

She pours herself wine.

So. I hear much of your rhetorical endeavours.

JEKYLL. I'm – I beg your pardon?

KATHERINE. It seems one can't avoid reports of learned papers given here, and published there. For the encouragement of social purity, and the imminent suppression of improvidence and casual vice among the feckless classes. I mean, this is clearly way beyond the purview of the Ladies' Sanitary Association.

JEKYLL. Well, I understand that you might find my efforts risible.

KATHERINE. No, not entirely. And quite definitely impressive.

JEKYLL. In quantity if not in quality.

KATHERINE. Considering the experience you've been through.

JEKYLL. What d'you mean?

KATHERINE. To have a friend – a man on whom you'd heaped so many generosities . . . To find yourself so grossly and maliciously deceived.

Pause.

JEKYLL. Well, yes.

KATHERINE. Do the police have any notion where he is?

JEKYLL. There's been no sign. He has no family and few familiars. They think he may have fled abroad or drowned himself.

KATHERINE. It is remarkable, here in England in the nineteenth century, that people can apparently just disappear. As if they'd never been.

JEKYLL. Indeed.

KATHERINE. From a wanted murderer, to someone like – that poor wee Annie.

Pause.

JEKYLL. Katherine, I must assure you, there was nothing poor nor in that sense particularly wee about Ann Loder. What there was about her was a fancy man.

KATHERINE. So you think that's why she's disappeared?

JEKYLL. It seems a plausible hypothesis.

KATHERINE. Still, odd she didn't leave a note. Unless of course she's actually in trouble.

JEKYLL. In which case –

KATHERINE. In which case, you're a doctor, she'd have turned to you.

Pause.

JEKYLL. Well, whatever the circumstances were, or weren't, she went. And she hasn't had the courtesy to let me know – or you know, for that matter – where she's gone or whom she's gone with. And so there it is.

KATHERINE. And we shall have to see.

JEKYLL. I beg your pardon?

KATHERINE. Nothing.

Slight pause.

And I must beg yours.

JEKYLL. Why?

KATHERINE. For oppressing you with talk of Annie Loder, and those demanding children. When you're here to rest in peace.

She realises her gaffe.

I mean to rest. And to be left in peace.

JEKYLL. In fact, I went for a long walk this afternoon. I think I saw the children skating past the farm.

KATHERINE. And on the day of rest.

JEKYLL. And peace there was. And rest I will.

Enter CHARLES.

CHARLES. Mama, nurse says –

KATHERINE. Oh, Charles.

CHARLES. – that cook says someone's called –

KATHERINE. Now, why aren't you in bed?

CHARLES. – who needs to see you urgently.

KATHERINE. Why cook?

CHARLES. Because he's in the kitchen.

Enter LUCY.

KATHERINE. And who is this 'someone'?

LUCY. Didn't say.

CHARLES. Perhaps a policeman.

LUCY. Or a long-lost distant relative.

KATHERINE. Well, we've no need of a policeman. And one hopes a relative, however distant, would come to the front door. Now go to nurse and go to bed. You will forgive me, Henry.

JEKYLL. Yes, of course.

KATHERINE *goes out, followed by* CHARLES. LUCY *goes and finds the spinning top.*

LUCY. Uncle.

JEKYLL. Yes, what?

LUCY. Do you know what this is?

JEKYLL. No?

LUCY. It's the spinning top you brought me.

Pause.

JEKYLL. Lucy, I think your mother said –

LUCY. I painted it. I painted faces on each side. You see, one friendly, and one fierce.

Pause.

JEKYLL. And I'm sure –

LUCY. So when you spin it, first it looks like one man smiling and then frowning and then eventually they sort of merge. Would you like to see it, uncle?

JEKYLL *can't speak.*

Now just watch, when it starts to go, what happens.

She starts the top. JEKYLL *grabs it.*

Oh, uncle –

JEKYLL. You were told to go to bed.

LUCY. Yes, but –

JEKYLL. So you will do so *now.*

LUCY. But uncle –

JEKYLL. Now! This instant!

JEKYLL *is about to throw the top against the wall. He stops himself and places it on the floor.* LUCY *picks it up and runs out. A pause.* JEKYLL *goes to the side table where the wine is, picks up the decanter, and, to his surprise, pours himself a glass of wine. Then, equally to his surprise, he goes to the piano, sits, and begins to play, rather beautifully, a tune we might recognise. Then he hears a voice behind him.* KATHERINE *has entered.*

KATHERINE. Teddy?

JEKYLL *turns.*

KATHERINE. *Teddy?*

JEKYLL. What?

KATHERINE. Oh, I'm sorry, for a moment . . . Very strange. As if I saw . . .

Slight pause.

JEKYLL. Saw what?

KATHERINE. Saw nothing. There is nothing there. Trick of the light.

JEKYLL. Trick of the mind.

She sees the drink.

KATHERINE. And I see that you changed yours, Teddy.

JEKYLL *stands.*

JEKYLL. Please don't call me that. No-one's called me that since I was sixteen.

KATHERINE. No. Fifteen and a half. As I have reason to remember.

She goes to replenish her drink.

And, since you ask, that was Annie Loder's father. Who's a brute in drink but he's soft enough when sober. And who has received a letter, from, as it happens, distant relatives in Hammersmith. To tell him they've seen Annie.

Slight pause.

She was pregnant. With no sign of course of any father, who had doubtless slipped off briskly when he heard the news. Which the distant cousins, were able to appreciate, because when they discovered her condition, they threw her out into the gutter. On the grounds of their respectability and decency, and that of their whole street.

Pause.

The letter was a warning, Henry. To alert old Loder, if his daughter came here, to her condition and her character. So he would have no truck with her. As they had had no truck. Following the good example of her generous employer Dr Jekyll.

JEKYLL. Um –

KATHERINE. You know that Lucy is in tears.

Pause.

JEKYLL. I had thought we had agreed . . . that it was past her time –

KATHERINE. And to think she thought you were in love.

JEKYLL. I beg your pardon?

KATHERINE. Lucy. Last summer.

JEKYLL. Katherine, I hardly feel this is appropriate –

KATHERINE. Appropriate? No, obviously not. But she is a child. And thereby sadly prone to inappropriate ideas and feelings.

Slight pause.

A tendency which I remember every time my head goes dizzy and my legs give way and I look into a mirror at what's staring back at me.

Pause.

Henry, what were you playing?

JEKYLL. Playing?

KATHERINE. Just now. I thought it was – that thing we used to play.

JEKYLL. I, uh – I, what?

KATHERINE. You know, that fiendishly elaborate duet. My bit went something like . . .

She plays the top half of the duet on the piano.

And yours went –

Singing against the playing.

And *one* and rest and two and *rest* and one and two and one and *rest* and one . . . Come on, you must remember.

JEKYLL. No. No, as I said, I haven't –

KATHERINE. – played a note for thirty years. Of course. Which is why perhaps I wanted to believe that you might play it now. But it must have been – just my imagination.

LUCY (*off*). Mama!

KATHERINE *stands.*

KATHERINE. Well, I must go and tuck the children up. If you wanted to, you could come and say goodnight. And tomorrow – we will take our photograph.

She goes out. A moment. JEKYLL goes and looks at the piano. He starts to try to play the bottom half of the duet.

JEKYLL. No. No, it's one and rest and *rest* and two and one and two and one and rest and *rest* . . .

He looks at his hands. Suddenly, in panic, to the mirror. JEKYLL looks at his face. It's all right. But there is something of HYDE *in his voice.*

A photograph. What would she see.

Pause.

Imagine.

LUCY *calls from off.*

LUCY. Uncle Henry!

Scene Sixteen

Railway Station and train. Smoke and gas jets. JEKYLL *sees a cheaply dressed young* WOMAN *in a hooded gown. He moves towards her, as if recognising her. We hear the* RAILWAY GUARD.

RAILWAY GUARD. All aboard for London. North east platform, London train!

JEKYLL. What, Annie?

A young PARSON *hurries across the platform. The blowing of whistles, the slamming of doors.*

JEKYLL. Annie?

The WOMAN *turns. It isn't* ANNIE. *She disappears. A carriage appears; The* PARSON *enters it and sits.* JEKYLL *stands on the platform.*

RAILWAY GUARD. Last call for Sherborne, Gillingham, Temple Coombe, Salisbury and Waterloo! Last call, the London train!

JEKYLL *hurries into the compartment. We are now inside the train, lit through its grimy windows from the platform. The* PARSON *has an open newspaper.*

PARSON. Good evening, sir.

JEKYLL. Good evening.

PARSON. Right on time.

JEKYLL. Indeed.

JEKYLL *sits as more whistles blow and the train leaves the station. It's no longer light enough to read, so the* PARSON *closes his newspaper.*

PARSON. May I ask, sir, if you're travelling far?

JEKYLL. To London.

PARSON. I but to Salisbury. And to return tomorrow.

JEKYLL. Is that so.

PARSON. I have a modest country living quite nearby.

JEKYLL. I'm glad of it.

Slight pause.

I mean, the countryside is most agreeable.

PARSON. There is no doubt about it.

Slight pause.

Indeed, one sometimes wonders, at the wisdom of our mad rush to the cities. One speculates, as to whether there is something of an essence in these – babylons – that wastes minds and bodies and corrupts the soul.

JEKYLL. Well, yes –

PARSON. You will forgive me if I ask, sir, but did you know the young woman on the platform?

JEKYLL. No.

PARSON. That's what I thought. Yet for a moment you appeared to recognise her.

JEKYLL. Yes. I was mistaken.

PARSON. One can only hope she was arriving not departing.

JEKYLL. Yes, indeed.

PARSON. For otherwise, it's hard to entertain a cheerful speculation on the purpose of her journey. A young woman of that class and mien. And the fate which may await her at its end.

JEKYLL. What do you mean?

PARSON. The innocent but eager country girl. The promise of a London situation as a nursemaid, undercook or governess. And the discovery – too late – of how brutally she's been deceived.

JEKYLL. I beg your pardon?

PARSON. The medical inspection by the doctor, guaranteeing her virginity. The belief perhaps that the examination is the actual seduction. Till, numbed by gin or chloroform, she confronts her actual seducer. And in the morning, through her tears, the realisation that she has lost what cannot be regained, that she has had done to her in half an hour what can never be undone, no, not for all the crying in the world. And for those who ply this loathsome trade, for the pimps and procuresses and most of all the libertines themselves; can any man of sensibility contest that hanging is too liberal a remedy?

And when one reads of the unspeakable outrages that are the daily digest of our periodicals; of casual assaults in front of laughing passers-by; of women drowning their own babies; men visiting their lusts upon their children; the bonds of nature

turned to shackles of the vilest cruelty . . . How can one then
reject entirely the conviction that there is something in the very
ether of the times . . . That as we hasten to the century's end, so
too we rush headlong towards . . .

The train has arrived in a station. The PARSON *has looked at
his travelling companion and seen a different man.*

To the irreversible destruction . . . of the very . . . human . . .

Pause. HYDE *looks at his hands.*

HYDE. Sir.

The PARSON'*s throat is dry.*

PARSON. Yes, sir.

HYDE. Sir, I beg of you one service.

PARSON. Name it, sir.

HYDE *looks at the* PARSON.

HYDE. Describe me.

Scene Seventeen

The Back Door of JEKYLL'*s house. Very late Sunday night.*
HYDE *is desperately trying to find a way in: presently he is
attempting to clamber up to a window.* UTTERSON'*s voice
appears from the darkness:*

UTTERSON. Well, if it isn't Mr Hyde.

HYDE. Uh, what?

UTTERSON *leaps out from the darkness with his cane.* HYDE
jumps down and attacks back. UTTERSON *produces a blade
from what we now realise is a swordstick. He has* HYDE *up
against the wall, the blade at his throat.*

UTTERSON. So Poole was right.

HYDE. Why, Utterson.

UTTERSON. You know me then.

HYDE. Well, by repute.

UTTERSON. Then you will know what happens next.

HYDE. Oh, yes. I do.

UTTERSON. I'm glad of it.

HYDE. It's this.

HYDE quickly dispossesses UTTERSON of the swordstick and has him up against the wall.

You should have brought a policeman. Or your wee pal Enfield, even. Eh?

UTTERSON. You damnable –

HYDE. What happens next is this. I have need of a certain substance that is presently located in a drawer that is itself located in the room beyond that door.

UTTERSON. And this is not the only door that's barred to you.

HYDE. Precisely. So, what happens next is that Gabriel trots round the corner to the front door, calls up Poole, and fetches them for me.

UTTERSON. 'Fetches them'. In whose name, for God's sake?

HYDE. Dr E. Henry Jekyll, who d'you think?

UTTERSON. That gentleman is out of town.

HYDE. Oh, Utterson. That gentleman is here.

Slight pause.

UTTERSON. What, Jekyll is in London?

HYDE. Jekyll's here.

Pause.

UTTERSON. Oh, no.

HYDE. Oh, yes.

UTTERSON. You mean, that you and Jekyll –

HYDE. Aye. You got it.

Pause.

UTTERSON. Where is he?

Pause.

HYDE. What d'you mean?

UTTERSON. I mean, where is he? You have obviously got your claws in him again. Is he kidnapped or imprisoned? Have you hidden him?

HYDE. All too effectively it seems.

UTTERSON. So then?

HYDE. You havena understood.

UTTERSON. What should I understand? That you are a notorious blackguard and assassin, whose description is in every police office in the land, and who has now if not the person then at least some lever of control –

HYDE. Control. Oh would I had.

UTTERSON. Over my dearest friend.

HYDE. Your what?

UTTERSON. My dearest and my closest friend.

HYDE. Your *closest* friend?

UTTERSON. Oh, yes.

HYDE. Oh, Utterson. You can't imagine.

He takes the sword from UTTERSON's *throat.*

Well there's no point in forcing you to go. You take ten paces, and you call the police, and then I'm done for.

UTTERSON. Yes.

HYDE. So I must set about my business, on my own account.

HYDE *sheathes the sword.*

UTTERSON. You know, sir, you cannot count your hours of freedom beyond twenty-four.

HYDE. That's all I need.

UTTERSON. How so?

HYDE. The time it takes for a letter to be written and delivered.

UTTERSON. Well, we'll see. Am I to have this stick returned?

HYDE. No you are not.

UTTERSON. Well, then. Goodnight, sir. And. I hope, goodbye.

UTTERSON *goes out.* HYDE *breathes deeply.*

HYDE. Oh, Utterson. Thank God, you can't imagine.

HYDE *goes out.*

Scene Eighteen

LANYON's *house. Tuesday. A single lamp and desk. Enter* LANYON *reading a letter.*

LANYON. 'At midnight then, please see your servants are at rest and be alone in your consulting room. You will have the drawer that you collected earlier from my laboratory. At that hour my agent will present himself to you, and I ask you to place the drawer and all its contents in his hands without delay. Oh Lanyon, please be assured, that the neglect of any of these stipulations, however it might try imagination, may bring about if not my death then at the very least the shipwreck of my reason. Your friend, E.H.J.'

Scene Nineteen

KATHERINE'*s house. Tuesday early evening.* KATHERINE *enters reading a letter. It's from* ANNIE.

KATHERINE. 'You will I hope forgive me, Mrs Urquart, but as maybe you can well imagine I am in a desperate state. I am so feared my master as he was is under the control of this young man who is responsible for my condition, at first I thought it must be blackmail for some youthful pecc – adillo or the like but then your brother was so changed I thought it must of been' – of been – 'something more a matter of the mind. Or even worse suspicions of phenomenas as lurk beyond the realms of earthly reason'.

KATHERINE *looks up, her brow furrowed. She reads on.*

'But whatever it may be I have no choice have I but to throw myself upon his mercy hoping against all hope whatever hold as my seducer has on him be loosed'.

KATHERINE *looks at the envelope.* LUCY *and* CHARLES *appear in their nightclothes. She looks at the envelope.*

Posted at 2 a.m. on Monday. With no county.

She looks back to the letter.

'P.S. I do beg your pardon if I sound a penny dreadful but my master knows the words the other says without he's told them'.

CHARLES. Mama. Is something wrong?

KATHERINE. Children. You must go to bed. Tomorrow morning, very early, we will go and find your uncle. For yes, yes, there is something very wrong.

Scene Twenty

LANYON'*s house. Tuesday midnight.* LANYON *sits waiting with the drawer at his desk. There is a knock.* LANYON *goes and calls through the door:*

LANYON. Hallo!

HYDE's *voice.*

HYDE (*off*). Hallo! That's Lanyon?

LANYON. Dr Lanyon, yes. Are you from Dr Jekyll?

HYDE (*off*). D'you have it?

LANYON. I repeat my question.

HYDE (*off*). Aye. I'm from Jekyll.

Slight pause.

LANYON. Yes, I have.

> LANYON *opens the door.* HYDE *bursts in with* UTTERSON's *swordstick unsheathed. He puts it to* LANYON's *throat.*

HYDE. Where?

LANYON. If you let me pass I'll get it for you.

HYDE. Quick, man, quick.

LANYON. You forget, sir, that I have not yet had the pleasure of aquaintance with you.

HYDE. Oh, that's the bother, is it? Well, my name is Hyde.

LANYON. What, Edward Hyde?

HYDE. Correct. And now mebbe you'll furnish me the drawer.

> LANYON *gets a drawer.*

LANYON. The drawer contains a version book, a graduated glass, some wrappers of white powder and a phial one quarter full of a turbid purple liquid.

HYDE. A *quarter*?

> HYDE *looks through the drawer in some alarm.*

LANYON. That is what I said.

HYDE. And this is all? You've no tampered with the drawer in any way?

LANYON. Of course not, sir!

HYDE. Of course. There was – there must have been – a spillage of some kind.

LANYON. So it would seem.

HYDE. And just – three doses left.

LANYON. Well, if you say so.

HYDE. Och, it's no matter. There will be replenishments. You did give Poole the note?

HYDE *pours a quarter of the remaining liquid into the glass.*

LANYON. I did. And now I have completed my instructions in this matter –

HYDE. – you will leave me be.

Slight pause.

LANYON. I'm sorry?

HYDE. You heard. You will leave the room, and in ten minutes, you'll return. By which time, I'll be gone.

LANYON. Sir, are you instructing me where I may and may not go in my own house?

HYDE. That's right. So, if you'd be so kind –

LANYON. Well, naturally, I'm your devoted servant, sir. But I have to say that once outside I shall immediately wake up my man and send him for the police.

HYDE. Oh, Hastie, mon, you'd no?

LANYON. Sir, I would be grateful –

HYDE. I'd a-thought from you, of all folk, a wee modicum of human sympathy –

LANYON. Why – why should you expect –

HYDE. You with your ain wee secret. You with you ain – what – 'youthful peccancy'? Or was that just too long ago?

Pause.

LANYON. How d'you know of that?

HYDE. Aha.

LANYON. I – I demand to know –

HYDE. Well, you leave me little choice. I'll show you.

He takes the draught.

One, two, three –

It hits him. HYDE *grunts and doubles up.*

Four, five –

He knocks over the lamp. In darkness.

Uh . . . seven . . . nine . . . eleven . . .

LANYON. Light, I'll find a –

HYDE. Dammit, dammit. Uh. Uh – twenty-one . . .

LANYON. I'll find a – here –

HYDE. Twenty-five – oh God in heaven – twenty-eight . . .

LANYON lights the lamp. JEKYLL stands there. He looks at his watch.

JEKYLL. Thirty.

LANYON. Jekyll.

JEKYLL. Is it?

He shuts the watch and looks at his face reflected in the cover.

And now you have beheld. And you know everything. And I am at the mercy of your oath. As you are of mine.

LANYON. Where have you been?

JEKYLL. I have been – hiding. I too have dwelt outside the circle, in the dark.

LANYON. So, you –

JEKYLL. So me.

Pause.

It was a woman? In your past?

LANYON says nothing.

JEKYLL. Oh, Lanyon. Let me tell you. There is no escape. Try as you might, you'll always fear to sleep, for fear of waking to the moment you remember it was not a dream.

For it is – oh Lanyon, it is indeed as if we dwell inside a ring of light, surrounded by a black infinity. And there are demons in the darkness, certainly, they clutch and paw, as the little circle of our peace and safety shrinks around us.

And what is worse, when we look into that darkness, and we see the demons, it's as if we're looking in a glass.

But, worst, is that in fact the monster is already in the circle, and within our walls. And as we lock our doors and bar our shutters tight, he is already in the room, he sits down with us by the fire, he listens to our fearful whispers and he mocks at us.

I mean to say. Imagine.

Pause.

LANYON. Oh, yes. I can.

Slight pause.

It was a woman in our household. And – a compromising situation. And so . . . she was dismissed. Without a character.

JEKYLL. And that is all?

LANYON. It is enough. But no. No, as I discovered later. She drank acid. Took three days to die.

Slight pause.

But I have always thought – I would have found ways to forgive myself eventually. Had she been the only one. Or even, had she been the last.

Slight pause.

Oh, yes. I can imagine. All too well.

JEKYLL *gives the swordstick to* LANYON.

JEKYLL. Give that to Utterson.

JEKYLL *goes out, leaving* LANYON *alone.*

Scene Twenty-One

JEKYLL*'s hall. Later the same night.* JEKYLL *enters carrying the drawer, followed by* POOLE, *dressed in nightclothes, carrying a lamp. There is food laid out on a round silver tray for* JEKYLL.

JEKYLL. Poole, you received my letter.

POOLE. Yes I did sir.

JEKYLL. And you followed my instructions?

POOLE. Yes, sir, but –

JEKYLL. What 'but'?

POOLE. Sir, the dispenser of Messrs Maw presents his compliments –

JEKYLL. For Christ's sake, man –

POOLE. – but regrets that he is presently unable to complete your order.

JEKYLL. Oh my God . . .

He puts down the drawer.

POOLE. However, he has sent word to an associate, who may be in a position to supply another sample of the potion –

JEKYLL. When, man, when?

POOLE. Which he hopes might be delivered at the opening of business in the morning.

JEKYLL (*looks at his watch*). What, today?

POOLE. Indeed, sir.

JEKYLL. When do they open?

POOLE. Eight o'clock I'd think sir.

JEKYLL. Then you will be there. Outside the shop. From half past seven on the dot. D'you understand?

POOLE. Yes, yes I understand –

JEKYLL goes and unlocks the laboratory door.

JEKYLL. Now leave me be.

POOLE. But, sir –

JEKYLL. Yes, what?

POOLE. It's just – I ought to, sir –

JEKYLL coming back for the drawer.

JEKYLL. Oh, spit it out, man –

POOLE. – say that if you are planning working late, sir, I should say, sir, that your – earlier associate was seen at the back door. On Sunday night. By me at first, and then, by Mr Utterson.

Pause.

JEKYLL. My 'earlier associate'.

POOLE. One must hope he will be quickly apprehended.

Pause.

JEKYLL. Yes, one must. Must hope, indeed.

JEKYLL picks up the drawer, and hurries to the laboratory door. As he goes through, POOLE remembers the food he prepared for his master.

POOLE. Sir, I prepared . . . in case you wanted . . . .

JEKYLL calls after.

JEKYLL. Goodnight, Poole!

JEKYLL slams the laboratory door behind him.

POOLE. I will see you in the morning, sir.

Scene Twenty-Two

Still JEKYLL's hall, in darkness. The sonorous four o'clock chime is joined by an insistent ringing of the front door bell. After a moment or two, JEKYLL hurries in from the laboratory, with his lamp. He is in his shirtsleeves and waistcoat. He nearly runs into POOLE, who appears, also with a lamp, from the front door, with a letter.

JEKYLL. Is that – from Messrs Maw . . .

POOLE. No, sir. It is a letter.

JEKYLL. Letter? Who from?

POOLE. It was delivered here by Dr Lanyon's valet, sir.

JEKYLL. Lanyon? I was with him but an hour ago.

POOLE. I think, sir, it was more like four.

JEKYLL. Four?

In alarm, JEKYLL *looks round for something shiny. He sees the food on the silver tray, sweeps it off, and holds it before his face. He looks the same.*

Give me the letter.

POOLE. Yes, sir. Certainly.

POOLE *takes the tray from* JEKYLL, *picks up a knife laid out with the food in lieu of a paperknife, and presents the tray with the letter to* JEKYLL.

Your letter, sir.

JEKYLL, *tearing the letter open.*

JEKYLL. Poole, this is no time –

POOLE *is putting the food back on the tray.*

POOLE. No, indeed not sir.

JEKYLL *has got the import of the letter.*

JEKYLL. Oh no.

POOLE. Bad news, sir?

JEKYLL*'s voice is thickening.*

JEKYLL. Bad? Bad news?

He recovers.

Yes. Yes it is. Four hours.

JEKYLL *makes quickly for the laboratory. Suddenly, he turns back and darts at* POOLE. *In fact, he's after the food. He almost pushes* POOLE *aside, grabs the tray, and hurries with it to and through the laboratory door, slamming it behind him.*

Scene Twenty-Three

JEKYLL*'s laboratory, a quarter to eight on a wintry morning. The windows are curtained. A single lamp illuminates the sleeping* JEKYLL *and the workbench, on which sits the final glass of purple liquid, in its graduated glass, on the silver tray, with the letter, the knife, and the remainder of the food.*

Through the gloom we can see that JEKYLL's *father's portrait stands in place of the mirror; the recesses of the room, including the area around the red baize door, remain in darkness.*

We hear the three-quarter chime, interrupted by a banging on the door. JEKYLL *wakes.*

JEKYLL. What? Poole? What time is it?

He runs to the red baize door and calls:

Is that you, Poole?

The banging starts again. JEKYLL *realises it comes from the back door. Picking up the knife on his way, he goes to the back door and calls.*

Who's there?

ANNIE (*calls from outside*). It be Annie, sir.

JEKYLL. Annie.

ANNIE (*calls*). Annie Loder, sir.

JEKYLL. What do you want?

ANNIE (*calls*). I wants to see you, sir.

JEKYLL. Annie, please go away.

ANNIE (*calls*). I won't go, sir. Least not as 'till –

JEKYLL. Annie, there's not time –

ANNIE (*calls*). – I sees your face, sir.

Slight pause.

JEKYLL. My face?

ANNIE. Thassit sir. And as you be you.

Quickly, JEKYLL *touches his face. He has not time to find a mirror. He goes and unbolts the door and unlocks it.* ANNIE *enters. She is as well wrapped as she can be against the cold.* JEKYLL *follows her back into the body of the room. She looks at him.*

JEKYLL. It's nearly light.

ANNIE. Yes, sir. Be nearby eight o'clock.

She goes to draw the curtains.

Does you want me to –

JEKYLL. No, no. No, really.

He goes and picks up the lamp, his back to ANNIE.

ANNIE. It be from the lick of lamplight at the window. As I knows you're back.

JEKYLL. I'm back?

ANNIE. See, I been a'calling by for days. Ever since I finds – as I got no place else to go.

JEKYLL turns, holding the lamp to show his face.

JEKYLL. Well, here it is. And I trust that 'it be me'.

ANNIE. Oh, sir . . .

JEKYLL. And now it is established that I am indeed myself, and not I trust a 'fiend . . . '

ANNIE (*almost crying with relief*). . . . 'fiend in human form . . . '

JEKYLL is finding money in his wallet.

JEKYLL. . . . . we'll see what can be done.

ANNIE. Uh – done, sir?

JEKYLL. Unfortunately, my staff are all away, and I myself am but in temporary residence. But, at least, I imagine . . .

She holds out the banknotes.

. . . you could 'use the ha'penny'.

ANNIE. Oh, sir.

She's crying.

JEKYLL. Now, please.

ANNIE. Oh, sir. It's just – to see you, here, now, in your normal self –

JEKYLL. There's really, there's no need –

ANNIE. And recalling how you was when we last met –

JEKYLL. Well, yes, I fear that I –

ANNIE. But now to see you back in your old character, and free of him . . .

JEKYLL can't not ask.

JEKYLL. I'm sorry? Free of who?

Slight pause.

ANNIE. I mean, sir, I do have such thoughts.

JEKYLL. I've no doubt. Free of who?

ANNIE. About – I'm sure you'll take it as a fancy – but as how he somehow works his way inside your head, that it be the – like the fellow with the speaking doll, or I'm sorry sir, I mean like hypnotism or how d'you say it like – tepelathy –

JEKYLL. Telepathy.

ANNIE. Or even – even –

JEKYLL. Yes? Or even?

ANNIE. Even –

JEKYLL. What.

ANNIE is beginning to sense something odd about JEKYLL.

ANNIE. But as I says, it just be a fancy. And whatever, it be all gone now. And I'm sorry to take up your time, sir, and thankee kindly I'll be on my way.

JEKYLL gestures her towards the back door. But ANNIE has seen LANYON's letter.

JEKYLL. Of course.

As ANNIE picks up the sense of the letter, JEKYLL goes back to his wallet, and finds a card to write on.

But look, Annie, if you find you are in need again, to save you coming here –

ANNIE has understood LANYON's letter, but thinks JEKYLL has written it.

ANNIE. Oh sir. What's this?

JEKYLL turns and sees what she's found.

JEKYLL. That is a private letter.

ANNIE. Oh, but sir.

JEKYLL. And as such nothing of your bus-

ANNIE (*reads the letter*). 'You showed me that a man cannot escape his past misdeeds.'

JEKYLL. Give me that letter.

ANNIE. 'And that a man *should* not.'

JEKYLL. I demand it. At this instant.

ANNIE. 'And as I have escaped the judgement of the world, so must I now exact it on myself.'

They both clock the significance of the glass of purple liquid at the same moment. ANNIE gets to it first.

JEKYLL. Annie.

ANNIE. No, sir.

ANNIE is backing away, holding the glass.

JEKYLL. Annie, please, I beg of you –

ANNIE. No, sir. I cannot – cannot let you, sir.

JEKYLL. But, no, it's not –

ANNIE. Whatever he may say, or whatever you maybe a-done, I cannot –

JEKYLL. It is – it is all I have –

ANNIE *throws the liquid away.*

ANNIE. So there, there be an end to it.

She stands, defiant. JEKYLL *doubles up in despair, his voice gruffening.*

JEKYLL. Oh, Annie. What. What have you done.

There's knocking at the red baize door.

Uh . . .

JEKYLL *goes quickly to the door.*

Yes? Yes, Poole?

POOLE (*calls*). Sir, I have been to the pharmacist as you instructed.

ANNIE (*to herself*). Poole.

In the darkness, we sense JEKYLL's *body beginning to change.*

JEKYLL. Yes?

POOLE (*calls*). But he regrets that his associate has not been able to secure a further sample of the drug –

JEKYLL. Oh God –

ANNIE (*to herself*). I thought you said . . .

POOLE (*calls*). – and indeed that he is unaware of any further source in London or indeed –

JEKYLL. What, anywhere?

POOLE (*calls*). – for which he is naturally most apologetic.

JEKYLL's *voice is thickening.*

JEKYLL. Uh . . .

POOLE (*calls*). Sir, is all well with you?

JEKYLL. Yes. All is very well.

POOLE (*calls*). And there's nothing else that your require?

JEKYLL. No, nothing else at all.

POOLE (*calls*). In that case, sir, perhaps . . . . I will make one more visit to the chemical suppliers. Just in case . . . . catastrophe may be averted.

Pause.

JEKYLL. Yes.

POOLE (*calls*). If that is all sir.

JEKYLL. Yes. That will indeed – be all.

His voice has changed. He turns, still in darkness. But we – and ANNIE *– can tell he is transformed.* ANNIE *runs to the back door. She tries to open the unbolted door. It won't open. She slowly turns. Holding up the key,* HYDE *walks into the light.*

HYDE. Beg pardon? Free of who?

A moment, then ANNIE *runs to the red baize door. It's locked. She is heading for the window when* HYDE *intercepts her, secures her and drags her down towards the workbench.*

Reet. A demonstration of the miracle of telepathic transference. What's pumping round wee Annie's brain.

HYDE *throws* ANNIE *down on the workbench. He kneels on top of her, one hand at her throat. With the other hand, he is preparing a potion.*

One. Question. Does anybody ken what she kens noo? And the answer: If the note is not *from* Henry Jekyll then it must be 'to'. As indeed it is. From his old pal Hastie Lanyon. Who we gather takes a servicably handy blade to his own throat between the hours of half past one and four o'clock this morning. While three, aye, Poole has doubtless worked out all's not well within. But by the time he's stottered round to Utterson and back I have to tell ye I will be long gone.

Slight pause. he looks into ANNIE*'s terrified face.*

As in a different sense will you. Because, wee Annie, you was right in one respect. There will indeed be a suicide in here this cold grey morn.

He lights LANYON*'s letter with the lamp and burns it.*

For four. Disconsolate at his friend Lanyon's death, Dr Henry Jekyll ups and offs to foreign parts unknown. Leaving for five the backdoor open – well, why not – through which bobs guess who Annie Loder, destitute and ruined, to find a note to Poole from her only possible deliverer explaining all. So six no wonder the poor hizzie's driven in a moment of distraction to abuse his hospitality. To do that thing that cannae be undone. No, not for all the crying in the world.

He places a glass of poison on the silver tray.

Which all adds up, my dear, to the only two folks know the
truth of the good doctor dead by their own hand. And E.H.J? In
Mexico. New Zealand. Or Natal. With his signature. Thereby
eighty thousand sterling. And lacking only that which nobody
will know. His face.

He lets this sink in a moment.

So, whatcha reckon?

ANNIE *bites* HYDE'*s hand, breaks free and jumps from the
workbench.*

Oh, Annie.

ANNIE *rushes to the baize door, bangs and shouts.*

ANNIE. Help! Help, Mr Poole!

No answer.

HYDE. I told you. On the road to Utterson.

HYDE *makes for* ANNIE. ANNIE *dashes back to the workbench.*

Oh no. Oh no.

ANNIE *and* HYDE *race for the workbench.* HYDE *gets the
knife,* ANNIE *grabs the salver, moving away.* HYDE *stalks*
ANNIE *upstage.*

Hm. Well. Now come on, Annie. There's nae way out. There's
no one by.

HYDE *closes in on her with the knife.*

So why no – just –

Suddenly, ANNIE *holds the silver tray up in front of her face.*

Uh – what –

He's taken aback.

What's this?

ANNIE. What do it look like, sir?

HYDE. What, you're trying to fright me with my ain – ain face?

ANNIE. No, sir. I wants to know whose face it be.

HYDE. 'Who's face it be'?

ANNIE. 'Cos I reckons when we gets the face, we get the name.
And when we gets that, we gets everything.

HYDE. The name?

ANNIE. Dr E. Henry Jekyll. Edward Henry Jekyll. Edward. Eddie.
Teddy.

She takes the tray down.

Yes?

With a horrible cry, HYDE *runs at* ANNIE *with the knife. At the last moment, she jumps aside, revealing* JEKYLL's *father's portrait, into which* HYDE *plunges his knife.*

HYDE. Ah . . . uh . . .

After a moment, HYDE *starts to stab and slash at the portrait, ripping great tears in it, grunting and howling and weeping. Finally, he comes to rest.* ANNIE *looks at* HYDE *and what he's done.*

ANNIE. Teddy. Three sizes smaller'n his pa. Teddy whose sister's only got one eye. Teddy who done so many things can never be undone, no not for all the crying in the world.

She turns and sits, her back to HYDE.

Well, as he do say. There's no way out. And no-one by. And here I be.

Slight pause.

The only person left who knows. The only person he can tell.

Pause.

So go on, Teddy. Tell me.

HYDE *doesn't move, for a long time. Then, slowly standing, he begins to speak.*

HYDE. You ken. You know. I thought that there would come a time. When I'd be finally declared . . . the chip off the old block. But . . . but it never came.

Slight pause.

ANNIE. So then . . .

HYDE. But rather, truth be told, it seemed that I was born, and would remain, beneath contempt. A fairground mirror, in which he saw himself distorted and half size.

Pause.

ANNIE. But . . . . but, for her . . .

HYDE. For her . . . Oh it was different.

Slight pause.

For her . . . who cheeked him, tweaked him, yattered at him, told him off . . . Oh, she could do no wrong. What smiles and sweet caresses. As I . . . stood by.

Slight pause.

ANNIE. So, then. What happens..

HYDE. What?

ANNIE. Be it a day time, or an evening?

HYDE. Evening.

ANNIE. And . . .

HYDE. And I waited on the landing.

ANNIE. Till . . .

HYDE. She came. All decked up in her dawtie party frock . . . with her hair all bunched and bowed.

ANNIE. And how . . .

HYDE. And how she squealed, when I leapt out at her.

Slight pause. HYDE *picks up the poison, and comes forward, to stand behind* ANNIE.

And how she shrieked . . . as I pushed and pulled and mussed her hair. And tore, and slashed and spat at her. And when . . .

ANNIE. And when . . .

HYDE *kneels and puts his forearm across* ANNIE'*s throat.*

HYDE. And when I took her ringlets in my fists . . . and dragged her to the bannister, and smashed her head down on the upper post . . . and heard the dead crack of the sincipital bone . . . Oh how she screamed.

Pause.

ANNIE. And be . . . be that the worst.

HYDE. No, no. Far worse than that, the worst of all, was when the grown-ups ran upstairs, and found her. And cried Katherine, what's happened? And she said, she'd fallen. And nobody was to blame.

Pause.

ANNIE. And so what's it feel like, Teddy? Like, inside?

Pause.

How d'you feel inside?

HYDE. Feel? Nothing. Empty. Void.

Pause.

ANNIE. Like a stain of breath upon the glass.

A knocking at the door.

UTTERSON (*off*). Hey, Jekyll, are you there?

HYDE. And *one* two three and *two* two three and *three* two three and one . . .

ENFIELD (*off*). Dr Jekyll, if you are in there, then for God's sake tell us!

HYDE *is singing the tune of the piano piece he played in Dorset.*

HYDE. And *one* and rest and rest and *two* . . .

UTTERSON (*off*). Jekyll, unless you answer, we will use brute force!

ENFIELD (*off*). And we are armed!

UTTERSON (*off*). And we are armed!

HYDE *lifts the poison. We think he is going to force* ANNIE *to drink it.*

HYDE. . . . and one and two and one and *rest* and rest . . .

An axe hits the baize door. HYDE *drinks the poison..*

And three and rest and four and five . . .

Another axe blow.

. . . and rest . . . and three . . . and rest and two and rest . . . and one . . . and rest . . . I will.

As the door breaks open, HYDE *slides to the floor.* ANNIE *closes her eyes.* UTTERSON, *the armed* ENFIELD *and* POOLE *burst in.* ANNIE *stands and moves a little away.*

ENFIELD. Jekyll?

POOLE. No, no. It is – the other.

UTTERSON *to the body as* ENFIELD *searches with his revolver. No-one pays any attention to* ANNIE.

UTTERSON. Dead. By a cyanide.

ENFIELD. There is another door?

POOLE. There is, but it's –

ENFIELD *has gone to the door.*

ENFIELD. Locked. From the inside.

UTTERSON. So, then, presumably he died by his own hand.

The doorbell sounds in the house. POOLE *looks to* UTTERSON.

Go, Poole.

POOLE *goes.*

Annie, where's your master?

ANNIE *shrugs.*

ENFIELD. Annie, was your master here?

ANNIE. Oh, yes, sir. He be here.

ENFIELD*'s seen the cut portrait.*

ENFIELD. Good God. What's that?

UTTERSON. It – it's his father . . .

ENFIELD *stops him with a gesture.* KATHERINE *stands in the doorway.*

KATHERINE. Where is he? What has happened?

UTTERSON. Madam –

KATHERINE *comes in, with* LUCY, CHARLES *and* POOLE. UTTERSON *gestures to* POOLE *about the children.* POOLE *doesn't know what to do.*

KATHERINE. I am Katherine Urquart. Where's my brother?

UTTERSON. Mrs Urquart, I'm afraid, your brother is not here.

ENFIELD. And surely, for your children, it is hardly fit –

KATHERINE *has seen the portrait.* POOLE *makes to take the* CHILDREN *out.*

KATHERINE. No, let them be. He was their uncle.

UTTERSON. Mrs Urquart, we have as yet no cause to think –

KATHERINE (*nodding at the portrait*). As yes, the picture is his father. That is – or that was – Edward Jekyll.

She goes and kneels by the body.

As this –

UTTERSON. – is Edward Hyde.

KATHERINE *looks at the body. Then she looks up at* ANNIE, *who nods.*

KATHERINE. No. This is Edward Henry Jekyll, Mr Utterson.

Pause. We begin to hear the music of the duet that KATHERINE *and* JEKYLL *played at Dorset.*

UTTERSON. What?

ENFIELD. I thought you said . . .

KATHERINE *holds up the head of the body. It is* JEKYLL*'s face.*

UTTERSON. Good lord above.

KATHERINE. Well, yes. Indeed.

Slight pause.

POOLE. But surely, sir, it can't be, that my master was –

KATHERINE. Oh, yes it is.

Pause.

UTTERSON. Then, it seems that I have lost within the space of half a day two friends I have but slightly known.

KATHERINE. Oh, sir, you must not believe you are alone in that. You are not the only one who should have seen. God knows, I should have. Long ago.

KATHERINE *looks up at the portrait.*

It was his father's notebooks. He was frightened. But he was a Jekyll, so of course no-one must see.

She cradles her brother's body.

Oh, Teddy, Teddy. Now it's all too late. We're here.

The music of the duet swells. The lights fade.